Azure: Microsoft Azure Administrator (AZ-104) Practice Tests

Your One-Stop Solution to Pass

the Microsoft Azure Administrator Certification Exam

Adenn Young

Table of Contents

Exam AZ-104 Microsoft Azure Administrator practice exam - Practice Test #1

Question 1:

You are an IT Manager for Contoso Electronics.

Recently you have received more requests to allow employees to Work From Home (WFH). You need to ensure that proper security measures are implemented when setting-up WFH access.

Contoso Electronics use Azure Active Directory to provide authentication for cloud services.

Which of the following options should you implement to ensure correct authorisation is granted only for those resources to which each user requires access?

(Select 4.)

1. Single Sign On (SSO)
2. Multi-Factor Authentication
3. Office 365 Password Expiration
4. Azure AD Connect
5. Role-based access control
6. Windows Autopilot
7. Conditional Access Policies

Explanation

Correct Answer(s): 1, 2, 5 and 7

Single Sign On (SSO)

Multi-Factor Authentication

Role-based access control

Conditional Access Policies

The explanation for the correct answers are:

Single Sign On can be implemented to ensure a single identity is able to access multiple resources. This will reduce the requirement for multiple usernames and passwords to access resources such as SaaS applications. SSO can be combined with other features of Azure AD such as Multifactor Authentication (MFA) and Conditional Access Policies (CAP) to provide additional security measures that protect the identity

https://docs.microsoft.com/en-us/azure/active-directory/manage-apps/what-is-single-sign-on

Multifactor Authentication is a security feature that requires an additional form of identification to validate the identity that is requesting access. There are three principals to MFA:

Something you know, typically a password.

Something you have, such as a trusted device that is not easily duplicated, like a phone or hardware key.

Something you are - biometrics like a fingerprint or face scan.

https://docs.microsoft.com/en-us/azure/active-directory/authentication/concept-mfa-howitworks

An Office 365 Policy enforces the criteria to which users must adhere when creating, or changing a password within Office 365.

https://docs.microsoft.com/en-us/microsoft-365/admin/misc/password-policy-recommendations?view=o365-worldwide

Azure AD Connect is a tool used to synchronize your On-Premises Active Directory accounts to Azure AD creating a hybrid identity scenario. This ensures that your users will use the same username and password to access resources both on premises and in Azure AD.

https://docs.microsoft.com/en-us/azure/active-directory/hybrid/whatis-hybrid-identity

Role-based Access Control – Roles are able to be set to specific identities, which in turn can then be used to map to specific Azure service instances.

https://docs.microsoft.com/en-us/azure/role-based-access-control/overview

Windows Autopilot is a service that can be used to pre-configure new devices to ensure that once a user logs in that device is configured for their use with a specific collection of apps.

https://docs.microsoft.com/en-us/windows/deployment/windows-autopilot/windows-autopilot

Conditional Access Policies (CAP) provide rules and conditions for which the identity must comply with to successful authenticate and be authorized access to resources in Azure.

https://docs.microsoft.com/en-us/azure/active-directory/conditional-access/overview

Review this website for additional information:

https://docs.microsoft.com/en-us/learn/modules/intro-to-security-in-azure/3-identity-and-access

Question 2:

A member of the DevOps team, DevUser1, is given a Owner permission of a Resource Group named CycleRG1, and all the Virtual Machines in the group.

A deny assignment is being applied to DevUser1, to deny deletion of Virtual Machines.

Review the following statement:

DevUser1 will be allowed to delete the any Virtual Machine resources from CycleRG1 because DevUser1 has Owner permission.

Is the statement True or False?

1. FALSE
2. TRUE

Explanation

Correct Answer(s): 1

FALSE

The explanation for the correct answer is:

With Azure Active Directory Role-based access control (RBAC) deny assignments block users from performing specified actions even if a role assignment grants them access.

A deny assignment is being applied which will stop the deletion of the Virtual Machines in CycleRG1 by DevUser1.

Deny assignments take precedence over role assignments. therefore DevUser1 will not be allowed to delete the VM.

Review this website for additional information:

https://docs.microsoft.com/en-us/azure/role-based-access-control/overview#deny-assignments

Question 3:

You are the IT Manager for Contoso Electronics, which has offices across the world. Due to varying time zones it is important that users are able to reset their own passwords without intervention from the IT Helpdesk.

You need to enable Self-Service Password Reset (SSPR) through the Azure portal.

You have already enabled SSPR within Azure Active Directory. Which three other steps do you also need to configure?

1. Open the Azure Portal, Select Security and enable MFA
2. Specify whether users are required to register for self-service password reset and how often they are asked to reconfirm their authentication method
3. Choose whether to notify users and/or all admins of password resets
4. Choose whether users are required to have one or two authentication methods and choose which authentication methods are allowed
5. Choose who to enable self-service password reset for, whether individual users or a security group

Explanation

Correct Answer(s): 2, 3, 4

Specify whether users are required to register for self-service password reset and how often they are asked to reconfirm their authentication method

Choose whether to notify users and/or all admins of password resets

Choose whether users are required to have one or two authentication methods and choose which authentication methods are allowed

The explanation for the correct answer is:

Self-Service Password Reset allows users to change their own password via a web portal, without the IT Helpdesk.

You can then use additional features such as Password Writeback which writes changes from the Cloud back to your on-premises AD environment.

Review this website for additional information:

https://docs.microsoft.com/en-us/learn/modules/allow-users-reset-their-password/3-implement-azure-ad-self-service-password-reset

Question 4:

To create and assign Azure Role Based Access (RBAC) you require the Microsoft.Authorization/roleAssignments/* permission.

Select which Azure Active Directory Roles grant Microsoft.Authorization/roleAssignments/* permission?

Choose all that apply.

1. Owner
2. Security Reader
3. Conditional Access Administrator
4. Virtual Machine Contributor
5. User Access Administrator

Explanation

Correct Answer(s): 1, 5

Owner

User Access Administrator

The explanation for the correct answer is:

Microsoft.Authorization/roleAssignments/* is granted with the Owner and User Access Administrator roles.

Security Reader is a role used for viewing security reports in Azure.

Conditional Access Administrator is used for configuring Conditional Access.

Virtual Machine Contributor is used for managing Virtual Machines.

Review this website for additional information:

https://docs.microsoft.com/en-us/azure/role-based-access-control/overview

Question 5:

CycleShare.com has deployed a hybrid environment.

What is the requirement for client devices to be able to use Azure Active Directory Seamless Single Sign-On (Azure AD Seamless SSO)?

1. Azure AD Joined
2. Domain Joined
3. Windows 10 clients only
4. Windows 8.1 and Windows 10 clients only

Explanation

Correct Answer(s): 2

Domain Joined

The explanation for the correct answer is:

The requirement for Azure Active Directory Seamless Single Sign-On (Azure AD Seamless SSO) is that the client devices must be Domain Joined.

Azure Active Directory Seamless Single Sign-On (Azure AD Seamless SSO) automatically signs users in when they are on their corporate devices connected to your corporate network. When enabled, users don't need to type in their passwords to sign in to Azure AD, and usually, even type in their usernames. This feature provides users easy access to your cloud-based applications without needing any additional on-premises components.

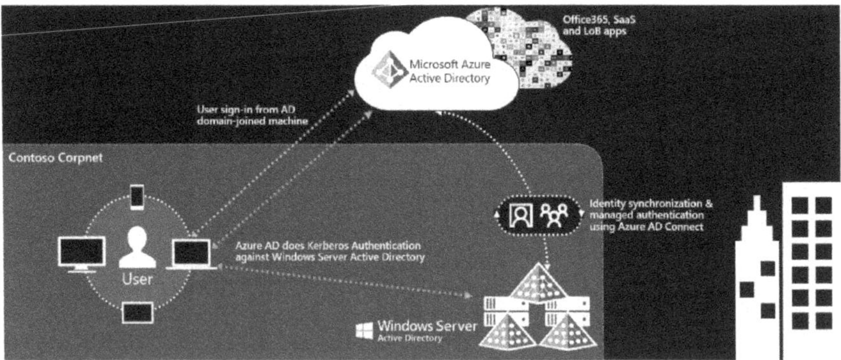

Review this website for additional information:

https://docs.microsoft.com/en-us/azure/active-directory/hybrid/how-to-connect-sso

Question 6:

You are a consultant working for CycleShare.com which uses Azure Active Directory.

Admin1 is a Global Administrator.

You notice that a group named Group1 contains several members that are Guest accounts.

You need to configure settings to ensure that Admin1 regularly checks that the list of Guest users within Group1 are still valid.

Select two options that you recommend?

1. Create an access review that is scoped to Guest users only
2. Use Privileged Identity Management (PIM) to review access
3. Use Privileged Identity Management (PIM) to approve pending requests
4. Create an access review that has selected users as reviewers

Explanation

Correct Answer(s): 1, 4

Create an access review that is scoped to Guest users only.

Create an access review that has selected users as reviewers.

The explanation for the correct answer is:

To review the list of Guest accounts in Group1, you should configure an access review that has a specified user/reviewer (such as Admin1).

The scope of the review needs to be set to Guest users only.

PIM is used for Azure AD administrative roles only, not groups, and approval is when someone asks to use their privilege, not to join a group/role.

PIM can review access to the built-in Azure AD roles and is not used for custom groups like Group1.

Review this website for additional information:

https://docs.microsoft.com/en-us/azure/active-directory/governance/access-reviews-overview

Question 7:

CycleShare.com uses Azure Active Directory.

You discover that several of your users are able to invite external users to view company online resources.

You need to prevent users from inviting external users in future.

1. Configure the 'Guests can invite setting' in the external collaboration settings.
2. Configure the 'Members can invite' setting in the external collaboration settings.
3. Configure the 'Members can invite setting' in the external collaboration settings.
4. Configure the 'Guest users permissions are limited' setting in the external collaboration settings.

Explanation

Correct Answer(s): 2

Configure the 'Members can invite' setting in the external collaboration settings.

The explanation for the correct answer is:

'Members can invite' is the setting that controls whether Azure AD users can invite external users to collaborate on Azure AD controlled resources.

The default setting is 'Yes'. To reduce unauthorized sharing you need to change this setting.

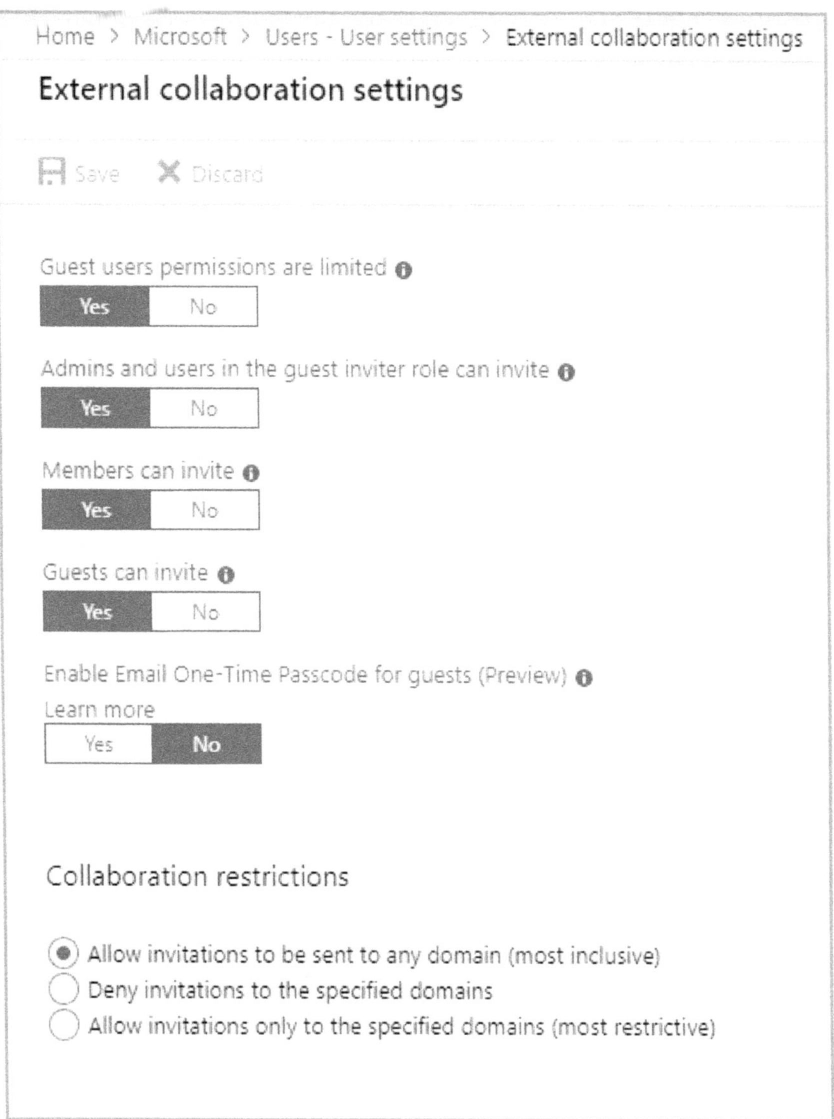

'Guests can invite' controls whether guest accounts can invite other guest accounts to resources.

'Guest user permissions are limited' controls the level of Azure AD access that guests can view.

Review this website for additional information:

Enable B2B external collaboration and manage who can invite guests https://docs.microsoft.com/en-us/azure/active-directory/b2b/delegate-invitations

Question 8:

CycleShare.com has contracted with external consultant Consult1 that needs access to some of your Azure resources.

Consult1 signs in to their device with their Azure AD user account but is unable to access your Azure resources

What should you do to ensure the contractor is able to access your Azure esources?

1. Your solution should not reduce security and minimize administrative effort.
2. Create a new user for Consult1 in Azure AD.
3. Add a new guest user in Azure AD for Consult1.
4. Configure the Multi-Factor Authentication settings for your Azure AD tenant.
5. Configure the LinkedIn account connections in Azure AD.

Explanation

Correct Answer(s): 3

Add a new guest user in Azure AD for Consult1.

The explanation for the correct answer is:

Adding a guest user for Consult1 in your Azure AD invites the current Azure AD user from the other tenant to that they can access CycleShare.com resources. Allowing Consult1 to be a guest user is preferential as this minimizes the security impact of allowing Consult1 to access your Azure resources.

Any user maintenance such as password resets are not managed by the CycleShare.com HelpDesk, so this minimizes administrative effort.

Creating a new user in your tenant would be unnecessary and require more maintenance, and reduces security.

Configuring Multi-Factor Authentication in your Azure AD tenant doesn't affect the account for the contractor as they should be an invited external user, not one of your user accounts.

Configuring Multi-Factor Authentication account connections in Azure AD allows users to connect to their work accounts with LinkedIn, but this doesn't provide the external contractor access to your Azure resources.

Review this website for additional information:

https://docs.microsoft.com/en-us/azure/active-directory/b2b/b2b-quickstart-add-guest-users-portal

Question 9:

CycleShare.com uses Azure Active Directory, Azure and Microsoft 365.

HelpDesk1 is a user within the HelpDesk team who joins Windows 10 devices to your Azure Active Directory.

The HelpDesk1 reports that she can no longer join new devices.

What should you configure?

1. In Azure Active Directory, configure the 'Maximum number of devices per user' setting.
2. In Azure Active Directory, configure the 'Users may join devices to Azure AD' setting.
3. In Azure Active Directory, configure the 'Require Multi-Factor Authentication to join devices' setting.
4. Apply the Device Enrollment Manager (DEM) role to the user.
5. Add the user to the Cloud Device Administrator role in Azure AD.

Explanation

Correct Answer(s): 4

Apply the Device Enrollment Manager (DEM) role to the user.

The explanation for the correct answer is:

You should apply the Device Enrollment Manager (DEM) role to the user account.

The user will then be able to enroll up to 1000 devices. A DEM account is useful for scenarios where devices are enrolled and prepared before handing them out to the users of the devices.

NOTE: If you don't use Microsoft Intune (which is included in Microsoft 365) you could configure the maximum number of devices that users can join, but this setting will also affect all users.

Requiring MFA to join devices is optional, but not required and doesn't affect the number of devices a user can join.

Changing the 'users may join devices to Azure AD' setting only affects which users can perform the task, not the quota.

Adding someone to the Cloud Device Administrator role provides them full access to manage devices in Azure AD, but not join new devices.

Configuring the maximum number of devices users can join is the correct answer, but it will also affect all users.

Review these websites for additional information:

https://docs.microsoft.com/en-us/intune/device-enrollment-manager-enroll

https://docs.microsoft.com/en-us/azure/active-directory/devices/device-management-azure-portal

Question 10:

CycleShare.com uses Azure Active Directory (AAD)

You have a group related to an obsolete project that has been used to receive emails in Exchange Online.

The group is now obsolete and you want the group to automatically be deleted in 180 days time.

What should you configure?

1. In Azure Active Directory, configure the Exchange administrator role in Privileged Identity Management.
2. In Azure Active Directory, configure a conditional access policy for Exchange online.
3. In Azure Active Directory, configure the Office 365 Group Expiration Policy.
4. In Azure Active Directory, configure an access review for the group.

Explanation

Correct Answer(s): 3

In Azure Active Directory, configure the Office 365 Group Expiration Policy.

The explanation for the correct answer is:

Office 365 Groups can be set to expire after a certain interval. Owners are notified before this occurs at 30 days, 15 and 1 day prior to removal.

If it is not renewed by an owner it will be automatically deleted after the expiry interval.

Privileged Identity Management won't allow automated deletion of a group, but it can be used to manage memberships.

Conditional Access Policies are used for access to cloud apps, and don't have a group expiry capability.

Access Reviews can be used to manage group memberships, but not deletion of groups.

Review this website for additional information:

https://docs.microsoft.com/en-us/azure/active-directory/users-groups-roles/groups-lifecycle

Question 11:

CycleShare.com uses Azure Active Directory.

You need to recommend an Azure Active Directory group type that allows you to assign access to a SharePoint Online document library.

You need to assign the membership based on the company department where the user is employed.

CycleShare.com has the following departments:

-Sales

-Marketing

-Administration

What should you recommend?

1. An Office 365 group type with assigned membership.
2. An Office 365 group type with a dynamic membership rule.
3. A security group type with a dynamic membership rule.
4. A security group type with assigned membership.

Explanation

Correct Answer(s): 2

An Office 365 group type with a dynamic membership rule.

The explanation for the correct answer is:

Office 365 groups allow access to SharePoint Online.

Using a dynamic membership rule which is based on Azure AD attributes such as "department" the membership of the Office 365 group can be automatically populated.

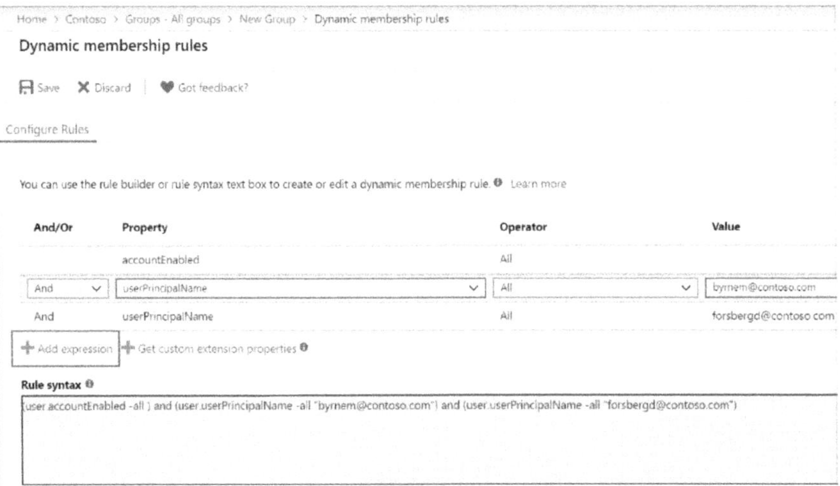

Review this website for additional information:

https://docs.microsoft.com/en-us/azure/active-directory/users-groups-roles/groups-create-rule

Question 12:

You need to create a new cloud user from the Azure Active Directory (Azure AD) portal.

You select "New User" and launch the "Create User" wizard.

From the list below, what properties can you configure?

Select all that apply.

1. Profile
2. Devices
3. Sync Settings
4. Licenses
5. Directory Role
6. Groups
7. Group Membership
8. Roles

Explanation

Correct Answer(s): 6, 8

Groups

Roles

The explanation for the correct answer is:

You can configure the following properties:

Groups

Roles

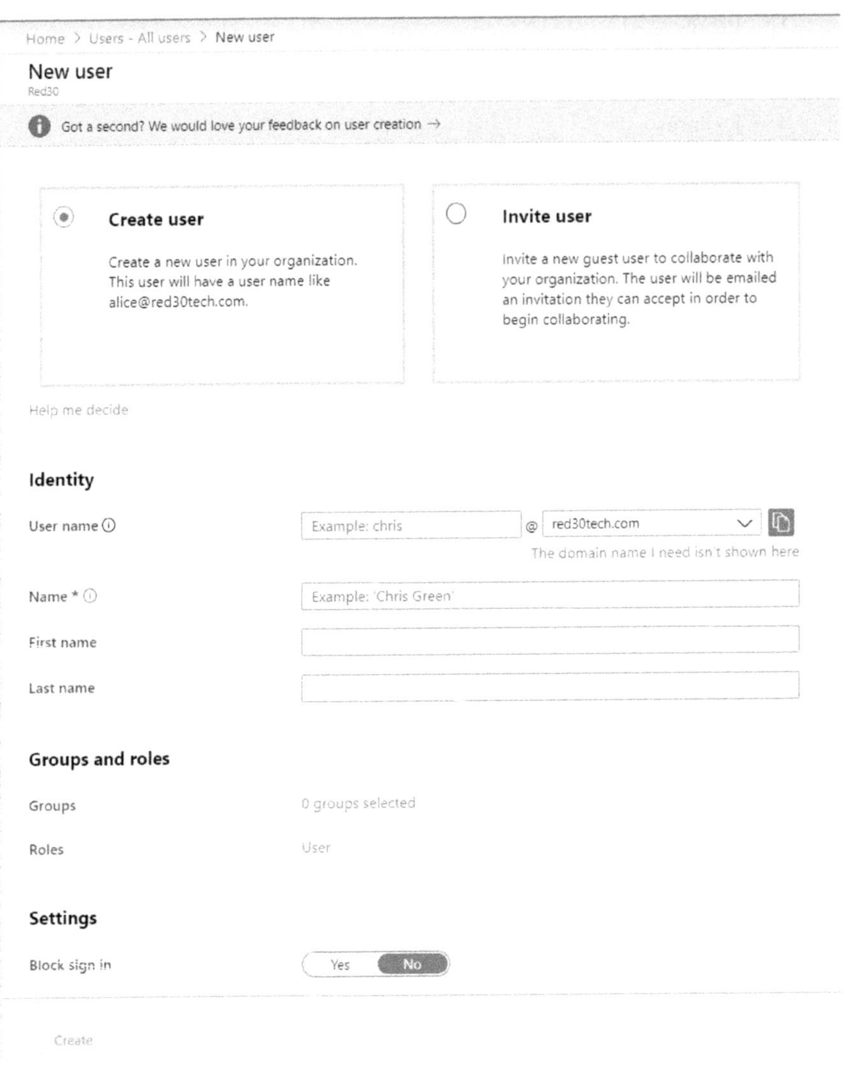

Review this website for additional information:

https://docs.microsoft.com/en-us/azure/active-directory/fundamentals/add-users-azure-active-directory

Note that this reference may need to be updated to the latest portal changes.

Question 13:

You are the Desktop Administrator for CycleShare.com.

Several users complain that they have to provide Azure Active Directory credentials every time they access company resources.

You need to improve the user experience and security of the Windows 10 client devices.

You need to check the device registration state.

What command must you run first?

1. ipconfig /flushdns
2. devmgmt.msc
3. dsregcmd.exe /status
4. psexec -i -s cmd.exe

Explanation

Correct Answer(s): 3

dsregcmd.exe /status

The explanation for the correct answer is:

The command line tool that provides troubleshooting information is dsregcmd.exe /status.

However, the dsregcmd.exe command needs to run as System, so you first need to run the psexec -i -s cmd.exe command to allow your commands running in the correct context.

Once you use dsregcmd.exe /status the tool which will check the device registration status for Windows 10 devices.

+--+

| Device State |

+--+

AzureAdJoined : YES

EnterpriseJoined : NO

DomainJoined : YES

DomainName : CYCLESHARE

+--+

ipconfig /flushdns will flush the DNS settings for the host.

Running devmgmt.msc will open device manager for the host.

adregcmd.exe /status is not a valid command in Windows 10.

Review this website for additional information:

https://docs.microsoft.com/en-us/azure/active-directory/devices/faq#q-how-do-i-know-what-the-device-registration-state-of-the-client-is

Also use this site for troubleshooting devices using the dsregcmd command:

https://docs.microsoft.com/en-us/azure/active-directory/devices/troubleshoot-device-dsregcmd

Question 14:

You are the Cloud Administrator of CycleShare.com which is a large organisation with multiple sites across the world.

The Sales Director asks you if there is anyway her team can reset their passwords while working away from the office without awaiting for the Helpdesk to respond.

The Helpdesk are available during US business hours.

You decide to implement Azure Active Directory Self-Service Password Reset (SSPR) but your Security Manager has concerns that this will introduce a security weakness to the CycleShare.com environment.

What approach should you use that will enable the Sales Team to reset their passwords while travelling and also ensure that no security weaknesses are introduced to the CycleShare.com environment?

1. Configure Self-Service Password Reset with the following settings:

   The number of methods required to reset are set to three.

   The methods used to reset are Mobile App code, Email and Security Questions.

   Enable this for the "Sales Team" only.

2. Configure Self-Service Password Reset with the following settings:

   The number of methods required to reset are set to two.

   The methods used to reset are Mobile App code and Security Questions.

Enable this for the "Sales Team" only.

3. Configure Self-Service Password Reset with the following settings:

   The number of methods required to reset are set to two.

   The methods used to reset are Mobile App code and SMS text.

   Enable this for the "All Users".

4. Configure Self-Service Password Reset with the following settings:

   The number of methods required to reset are set to three.

   The methods used to reset are Mobile App code, Email and SMS text.

   Enable this for the "All Users".

Explanation

Correct Answer(s): 2

Configure Self-Service Password Reset with the following settings:

The number of methods required to reset are set to two.

The methods used to reset are Mobile App code and Security Questions.

Enable this for the "Sales Team" only.

The explanation for the correct answer is:

SSPR can only be setup with a maximum of two methods.

The securest methods are Mobile App code and Security Questions then email.

Text SMS is the least secure method.

SSPR should be enabled for the Sales Team rather than the whole company and in this way, the security exposure is reduced.

Review this website for additional information:

https://docs.microsoft.com/en-gb/azure/active-directory/authentication/concept-sspr-howitworks

Question 15:

You notice that on a Resource Group named RG3, there are deny assignments configured in the Access Control (IAM) blade.

Your organization wants to protect newly deployed resources from being tampered with, even by an account with the Owner role.

How should deny assignments be defined?

1. Deny assignments are implemented through the use of the Azure portal.
2. Deny assignments are implemented through the use of Azure CLI.
3. Deny assignments are implemented through the use of Azure Blueprints.
4. Deny assignments are implemented through the use of Azure PowerShell.

Explanation

Correct Answer(s): 3

Deny assignments are implemented through the use of Azure Blueprints.

The explanation for the correct answer is:

To add a deny assignment, you use Azure Blueprints resource locks. Unlike regular RBAC assignments which can be implemented in the portal or via command line, you first need to create a blueprint definition.

With Azure Blueprints resource locks, you can protect newly deployed resources from being tampered with, even by an account with the Owner role. You can add this protection in the blueprint definitions of resources created by a Resource Manager template artifact.

The process is as follows:

- Create a blueprint definition

- Mark your blueprint definition as Published

- Assign your blueprint definition to an existing subscription

- Inspect the new resource group

- Unassign the blueprint to remove the locks

Deny assignments are created and managed by Azure to protect resources. Azure Blueprints use deny assignments to protect system-managed resources and are the only way that deny assignments can be created.

You can't directly create your own deny assignments.

Review this website for additional information:

https://docs.microsoft.com/en-gb/azure/role-based-access-control/deny-assignments

https://docs.microsoft.com/en-gb/azure/governance/blueprints/tutorials/protect-new-resources

Question 16:

You need to move a Virtual Machine from one Resource Group to another.

You decide to do this using PowerShell and the Move-AzResource cmdlet.

What parameters do you need to specify in order for the move to be successful?

Choose all that apply.

1. SourceResourceName
2. ResourceName
3. DestinationResourceGroupName
4. DestinationSubscriptionId
5. ResourceId

Explanation

Correct Answer(s): 3, 5

DestinationResourceGroupName

ResourceId

The explanation for the correct answer is:

In order to successfully move the resource between Resource Groups you will need the following script:

Move-AzResource -DestinationResourceGroupName "<myDestinationResourceGroup>" -ResourceId <ResourceId>

DestinationSubscriptionId is only required if moving between subscriptions.

SourceResourceName and ResourceName are not correct parameters.

Review this website for additional information:

https://docs.microsoft.com/en-us/azure/virtual-machines/windows/move-vm

Question 17:

Examine the following PowerShell script.

Set-AzResourceGroup -Name CycleShareRG -Tag @{ Dept="IT"; Environment="Test" }

What will be the resulting outcome of the script when it is run?

1. Apply the Dept tag as IT and the Environment tag as Test to the CycleShareRG Resource Group.
2. Deletes the Dept tag as IT and the Environment tag as Test to the CycleShareRG Resource Group.
3. Apply the Dept tag as IT and the Environment tag as Test to the CycleShareRG Resource Group. The script will overwrite any previous tags.
4. Displays the Dept tag as IT and the Environment tag as Test to the CycleShareRG Resource Group.

Explanation

Correct Answer(s): 3

Apply the Dept tag as IT and the Environment tag as Test to the CycleShareRG Resource Group.

The script will overwrite any previous tags.

The explanation for the correct answer is:

Every time you apply tags to a resource or a Resource Group, you will overwrite the existing tags on that resource or Resource

Group.

Review this website for additional information:

https://docs.microsoft.com/en-us/azure/azure-resource-manager/resource-group-using-tags

Question 18:

You manage the Azure subscription for CycleShare.com.

You want to be able to automatically assign a tag whenever resources are created in the Azure subscription.

What method would work best to enable this?

1. Setup auto-tagging to apply a tag to all created resources in the Azure subscription scope.
2. Configure an Azure Policy to apply a tag to all created resources in the Azure subscription scope.
3. Edit the "default resource tag" in the Azure subscription settings.
4. Apply the tag at the resource group and it auto-populate across resources within that group.

Explanation

Correct Answer(s): 2

Configure an Azure Policy to apply a tag to all created resources in the Azure subscription scope.

The explanation for the correct answer is:

Configure an Azure Policy to apply a tag to all created resources in the Azure subscription scope is the correct answer.

In Azure Policy, there are two built-in policies that are available to configure tags by default:

Apply tag and its default value: Applies a required tag and its default value if it's not specified by the deploy request.

Enforce tag and its value: Enforces a required tag and its value to a resource.

Auto-tagging is not possible.

Review this website for additional information:

https://docs.microsoft.com/en-us/azure/governance/policy/overview

Question 19:

What RBAC role do you need to assign to give Administrator access to an Azure subscription?

1. Administrator of the subscription
2. Security Owner of the Azure subscription scope

3. Owner of Azure subscription scope
4. Security Reader of the Azure subscription scope

Explanation

Correct Answer(s): 3

Owner of Azure subscription scope

The explanation for the correct answer is:

To make a user an administrator of an Azure subscription, assign them the Owner role (an RBAC role) at the Azure subscription scope.

The Owner role gives the user full access to all resources in the subscription, including the right to delegate access to others.

Review this website for additional information:

https://docs.microsoft.com/en-us/azure/billing/billing-add-change-azure-subscription-administrator#assign-a-user-as-an-administrator-of-a-subscription

Question 20:

Your DevOps Manager is unsure of a statement that he heard at a recent conference.

Applying a read-only Lock on a Resource Group with three Virtual Machines in it will prevent users from stopping or starting those VMs

Is this statement True or False?

1. TRUE
2. FALSE

Explanation

Correct Answer(s): 1

TRUE

The explanation for the correct answer is:

The statement is True - A ReadOnly lock on a resource group that contains a virtual machine prevents all users from starting or restarting the virtual machine. These operations require a POST request.

Review this website for additional information:

https://docs.microsoft.com/en-us/azure/azure-resource-manager/resource-group-lock-resources

Question 21:

Which of the following Azure Resources cannot be moved to another Resource Group?

Choose all that apply.

1. ExpressRoute
2. Data Lake Store
3. Traffic Manager
4. Logic Apps
5. Azure NetApp Files

Explanation

Correct Answer(s): 1, 5

Azure NetApp Files

ExpressRoute

The explanation for the correct answer is:

ExpressRoute and Azure NetApp Files cannot be moved across resource groups or subscriptions.

Traffic Manager, Data Lake Store and Logic Apps can all be relocated to another resource group or subscription.

Review this website for additional information:

https://docs.microsoft.com/en-us/azure/azure-resource-manager/resource-group-move-resources

Question 22:

When applying a tag to an Azure resource what two things do you need to supply?

1. Name and Region
2. Parameter and Field
3. Name and Value
4. Parameter and Value

Explanation

Correct Answer(s): 3

Name and Value

The explanation for the correct answer is:

To apply a tag to a resource in Azure you need to supply a Name and a Value.

The region will be automatically applied to a resource when you create the resource.

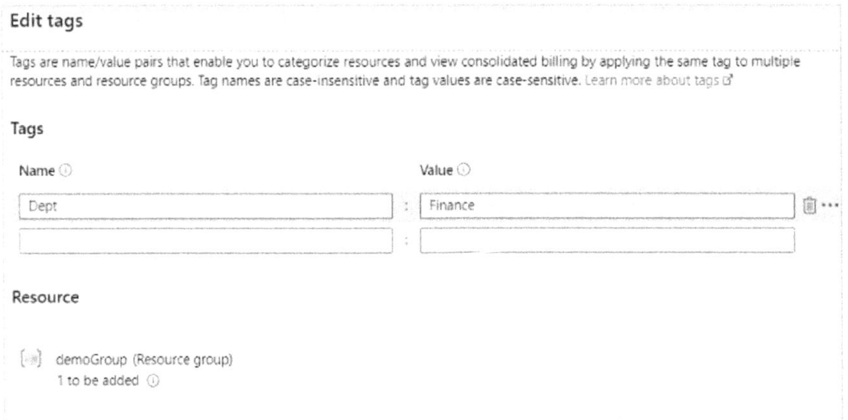

Review this website for additional information:

https://docs.microsoft.com/en-us/azure/azure-resource-manager/resource-group-using-tags#portal

Question 23:

Examine the following Azure tag names and select the one that would not be allowed as a valid tag name?

1. Development2
2. dev&test
3. MGMT-Approved
4. Project!

Explanation

Correct Answer(s): 2

dev&test

The explanation for the correct answer is:

dev&test is an incorrect tag name in Azure.

The following limitations apply to tags:

Not all resource types support tags. To determine if you can apply a tag to a resource type, see Tag support for Azure resources.

Each resource or resource group can have a maximum of 50 tag name/value pairs. Currently, storage accounts only support 15 tags, but that limit will be raised to 50 in a future release. If you need to apply more tags than the maximum allowed number, use a JSON string for the tag value. The JSON string can contain many values that are applied to a single tag name. A resource group can contain many resources that each have 50 tag name/value pairs.

The tag name is limited to 512 characters, and the tag value is limited to 256 characters. For storage accounts, the tag name is limited to 128 characters, and the tag value is limited to 256 characters.

Generalized VMs don't support tags.

Tags applied to the resource group are not inherited by the resources in that resource group.

Tags can't be applied to classic resources such as Cloud Services.

Tag names can't contain these characters: <, >, %, &, \, ?, /

Review this website for additional information:

https://docs.microsoft.com/en-us/azure/azure-resource-manager/resource-group-using-tags

Question 24:

Review the following statement and then decide whether it is True or False.

An Azure Resource Group is used for separating resources. Resources in the same resource group will be able to communicate freely as if in the same physical network.

1. FALSE
2. TRUE

Explanation

Correct Answer(s): 1

FALSE

The explanation for the correct answer is:

The answer is False. A resource group is simply a logical construct that groups multiple resources together so they can be managed as a single entity

Review this website for additional information:

https://docs.microsoft.com/en-us/azure/architecture/cloud-adoption/governance/resource-consistency/azure-resource-access

Question 25:

You have a Resource Group in your subscription named RG1.

You configure a tag on the subscription with the name Tag1 with a value of Value1.

You configure a tag on RG1 with the name Tag2 with a value of Value2.

You create a virtual machine named VM1 in RG1 and add the tag named Tag3 with a value of Value3.

You need to identify which tag or tags will be configured on VM1.

1. Tag1:Value1 and Tag2:Value2 and Tag3:Value3
2. Tag3:Value3 only
3. Tag1:Value1 and Tag2:Value2 only
4. Tag2:Value2 and Tag3:Value3 only
5. Tag2:Value2 only

Explanation

Correct Answer(s): 2

Tag3:Value3 only

The explanation for the correct answer is:

Tag3 will be the only tag to apply as tags do not inherit from parents such as resource groups or subscriptions.

Review this website for additional information:

https://docs.microsoft.com/en-us/azure/azure-resource-manager/resource-group-using-tags

Question 26:

You place a ReadOnly resource lock on a Resource Group that contains a virtual machine named VM3.

What is the effect of applying the resource lock?

1. You can delete VM3.
2. You can move VM3 to another Resource Group.
3. You cannot start VM3.
4. You can restart VM3.

Explanation

Correct Answer(s): 3

You cannot start VM3.

The explanation for the correct answer is:

A ReadOnly lock on a Resource Group that contains a virtual machine prevents all users from starting or restarting the virtual machine. These operations require a POST request.

This includes moving resources out to other resource groups, editing configurations of resources and in the case of virtual machines, changing their state from stopped to started.

A ReadOnly lock on a storage account prevents all users from listing the keys. The list keys operation is handled through a POST request because the returned keys are available for write operations.

A ReadOnly lock on an App Service resource prevents Visual Studio Server Explorer from displaying files for the resource because that interaction requires write access.

Review this website for additional information:

https://docs.microsoft.com/en-us/azure/azure-resource-manager/resource-group-lock-resources#how-locks-are-applied

Question 27:

You need to ensure that a tag named CostCenter1 is applied to all resources in Resource Groups in your Azure subscription.

These tags will help you to report billing information to each department in your organization.

What is the most effective way of implementing this?

1. Create an Azure policy in your subscription and assign it to each Resource Group.
2. Create an Azure policy in your subscription and assign it to the subscription.
3. Create a tag on one of the Resource Groups named CostCenter1 and assign a value.
4. Add the existing tag to other Resource Groups with different values.
5. Create a tag on one of the Resource Groups named CostCenter1 and assign a value.
6. Add the existing tag to other resources in each of the Resource Groups with different values.

Explanation

Correct Answer(s): 2

Create an Azure policy in your subscription and assign it to the subscription.

The explanation for the correct answer is:

Creating a Azure policy is the only way to guarantee that tags are enforced consistently across your subscription.

Manually assigning tags will not achieve your goal.

Assigning a Azure policy to Resource Groups would work for existing Resource Groups, but may not be adhered to in the future for new Resource Groups that are created.

You also need to ensure that the tags are assigned to each resource, not just the Resource Groups as they don't inherit.

Review this website for additional information:

https://docs.microsoft.com/en-us/azure/governance/policy/samples/enforce-tag-on-resource-groups

Question 28:

You need to recommend a solution that restricts the regions that administrators of your Azure subscription can use to deploy resources to.

What solution should you recommend?

1. On your Azure subscription, configure Usage + Quotas
2. Create an Azure policy and assign it to your Azure subscription.
3. On your Azure subscription, unregister Resource providers.
4. On your Azure subscription, add a budget.

Explanation

Correct Answer(s): 2

Create an Azure policy and assign it to your Azure subscription.

The explanation for the correct answer is:

Creating a policy that uses a definition that restricts the regions that you can deploy resources to is the only way to limit administrators.

Usage + Quotas is the part of your subscription where you can request an increase on the default quotas of resources each Azure customer is allocated.

Unregistering resource providers allows some restrictions on resources, such as virtual machines would not longer be available to deploy in your Azure subscription.

Budgets do not allow you to restrict where resources are deployed, they are used as a spending cost control tool.

Review this website for additional information:

https://docs.microsoft.com/en-us/azure/governance/policy/samples/allowed-locations

Question 29:

You have a user in your Azure AD tenant named User1.

User1 will be responsible for configuring the authentication methods in your Azure AD tenant.

You need to recommend which role to assign to User1.

Your solution should adhere to the principle of least privilege.

1. User Administrator
2. Global Administrator
3. Authentication Administrator
4. Security Administrator

Explanation

Correct Answer(s): 2

Global Administrator

The explanation for the correct answer is:

Only Global Administrators have the ability to modify the authentication settings in an Azure AD tenant.

Authentication administrators can only modify non-admin users.

Review this website for additional information:

https://docs.microsoft.com/en-us/azure/active-directory/users-groups-roles/roles-delegate-by-task#password-reset

Question 30:

You have a Resource Group named RG1 that contains 12 virtual machines.

You need a user named User1 to be able to start and stop virtual machines in RG1.

User1 must not be allowed to login to the virtual machines.

Your solution should minimize administrative effort where possible.

What should you configure?

1. On RG1, add a role assignment of Virtual Machine User Login to User1.
2. On RG1, add a role assignment of Virtual Machine Contributor to User1.
3. On each virtual machine in RG1, add a role assignment of Virtual Machine User Login to User1.
4. On each virtual machine in RG1, add a role assignment of Virtual Machine Contributor to User1.

Explanation

Correct Answer(s): 2

On RG1, add a role assignment of Virtual Machine Contributor to User1.

The explanation for the correct answer is:

To grant User1 the required level of access, you need to add a role assignment of Virtual Machine Contributor to User1.

The role assignment of Virtual Machine Contributor is sufficient without allowing them to login the VMs.

Assigning the role assignment at the Resource Group level will allow the assignment to be inherited to all the VMs in the Resource Group, thus minimizing the steps required.

You could also assign this role assignment directly on each VM, but it would require more administrative effort.

Review this website for additional information:

https://docs.microsoft.com/en-us/azure/role-based-access-control/built-in-roles

Question 31:

You have a resource group named RG1 that contains 12 virtual machines.

You need a user named User1 to be able to start and stop all of the virtual machines in RG1, except a VM named VM9.

Your solution should minimize administrative effort where possible.

NOTE: The requirement is to be assessed after ALL the actions have taken place.

What should you configure?

1. On RG1, add a role assignment of Virtual User Login to User1 On VM9 reset the password.
2. Move VM9 to another Resource Group. On RG1, add a role assignment of Virtual User Login to User1
3. Move all VMs to a new resource group except VM9. Add a role assignment of Virtual User Login to User1 on each VM in the new Resource Group.
4. Move VM9 to a new resource group. Add a role assignment of Virtual User Login to User1 on each VM in RG2.
5. On RG1, add a role assignment of Virtual User Login to User1. Move VM9 to another Resource Group.

Explanation

Correct Answer(s): 2

Move VM9 to another Resource Group.

On RG1, add a role assignment of Virtual User Login to User1.

The procedure should be performed in this order.

The explanation for the correct answer is:

The easiest approach to meet the requirement is to move VM9 out to another Resource Group and then assign the role on the existing resource group that contains the remaining VMs.

Modifying the password on VM9 is not the same as granting RBAC permissions in Azure.

Assigning roles more than once or granting the Virtual Machine User Login roles do not meet the goal, or minimize administrative effort.

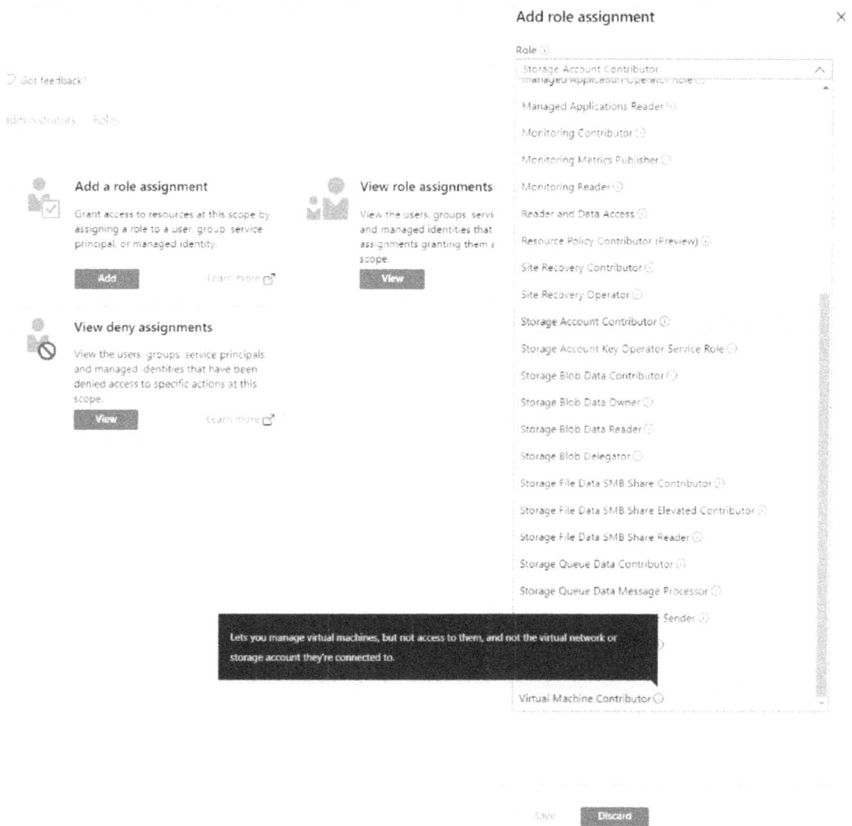

Review this website for additional information:

https://docs.microsoft.com/en-us/azure/azure-resource-manager/resource-group-move-resources

Question 32:

You have created a resource group named RG4 that contains networking resources such as virtual networks.

You need to create an Azure AD group named RGAdmins4 to be able to administer the resources in RG4, with the exception of the management of role assignments.

Which role assignment should you assign to RGAdmins4?

1. Contributor
2. Network Contributor

3. Owner
4. Reader

Explanation

Correct Answer(s): 1

Contributor

The explanation for the correct answer is:

Although RG4 contains network related resources, the requirement is to be able to administer any resource in RG4, so assigning the Contributor role is correct, rather than the Network Contributor.

Owner role would allow for role assignments to be changed which is stipulated that they should not be able to perform.

The Reader role would not allow changes to be made to any resource in RG4 at all.

Review this website for additional information:

https://docs.microsoft.com/en-us/azure/role-based-access-control/built-in-roles#contributor

Question 33:

You have a Resource Group called "VIPService7".

VIPService7 contains some very important Servers and a production Azure SQL Database.

You need to protect all resources in this Resource Group from deletion, whilst allowing staff to be able to modify the VMs if required and manage the database.

What solution would allow you to best do this?

1. Apply a Read-Only Lock to the Resource Group
2. Apply a Delete Lock to the Resource Group
3. · Remove all permissions from the Resource Group so only you have access
4. Apply a No-Delete Lock to the Resource Group

Explanation

Correct Answer(s): 2

Apply a Delete Lock to the Resource Group

The explanation for the correct answer is:

Applying a Delete Lock allows authorized users to still read and modify a resource, but they can't delete the resource.

ReadOnly allows authorized users to read a resource, but they can't delete or update the resource. Staff still need to be able to change the VMs and database.

Removing all permissions would not allow other staff to perform tier duties.

There isn't a setting called "No-Delete" Lock.

Review this website for additional information:

https://docs.microsoft.com/en-us/azure/azure-resource-manager/resource-group-lock-resources

Question 34:

You manage two Azure subscriptions CycleShare1 and CycleShare2.

You deploy 12 resources for a project into a Resource Group named RG1 on CycleShare1.

The resources contain no data, but you realize that you have deployed them to the wrong subscription.

Which action should you perform to ensure that the resources are associated to the CycleShare2 subscription?

1. Delete the resources in CycleShare1 and recreate them in the CycleShare2 subscription.
2. Download a template from Resource Group RG1 and use it to deploy the resources again to the CycleShare2 subscription.
3. Move the Resource Group RG1 between subscriptions.
4. Download a template for each of the 12 resources and deploy them in the CycleShare2 subscription.

Explanation

Correct Answer(s): 3

Move the Resource Group RG1 between subscriptions.

The explanation for the correct answer is:

It is possible to move Resource Groups and their associated resources directly between subscriptions.

This preserves any data and configurations and is the simplest way to achieve the goal.

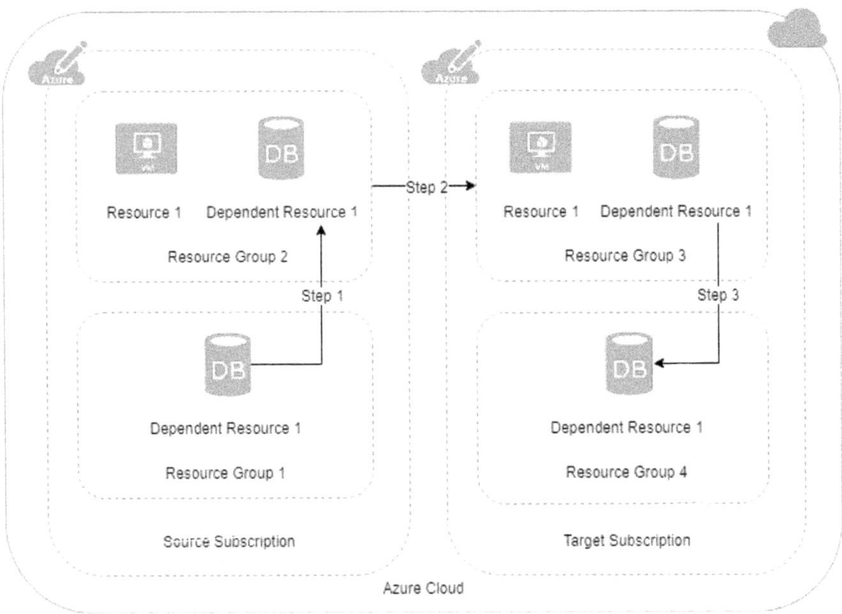

Deploying new resources from templates would work, but incur more administrative effort and would only reflect the resources configurations, not any existing data.

Review this website for additional information:

https://docs.microsoft.com/en-us/azure/azure-resource-manager/resource-group-move-resources

Question 35:

You are viewing the Access Control (IAM) blade of a Resource Group in the Azure portal.

You attempt to remove one of the role entries, but you are not successful.

What is the most likely reason that you cannot remove the entry?

1. The role assignment is configured at the subscription level and would need to be removed at that level.
2. The role is a Reader Role and cannot be removed.
3. There is a Delete Lock on the Resource Group.
4. There are Tags configured on the Resource Group.

Explanation

Correct Answer(s): 1

The role assignment is configured at the subscription level and would need to be removed at that level.

The explanation for the correct answer is:

If a Role Assignment is inherited from a higher level, it cannot be removed from the lower level. It can only be removed from the level it was configured at.

Reader Roles do not operate any differently to other types of roles.

Delete Locks do not affect the ability to remove RBAC assignments.

Tags do not affect RBAC assignments.

Review this website for additional information:

https://docs.microsoft.com/en-us/azure/azure-resource-manager/resource-group-move-resources

Question 36:

You have a user named Admin1 that is a member of several administrative groups in your Azure AD.

You examine the Access Control (IAM) blade on a Resource Group.

You need to enumerate which role assignments Admin1 has on the Resource Group.

How should you proceed?

1. View the Classic Administrators tab.
2. View the Check Access tab.
3. View the Roles tab
4. View the Role Assignments tab.

Explanation

Correct Answer(s): 2

View the Check Access tab.

The explanation for the correct answer is:

The Check Access tab allows you to query for a given user, group or service principal the role assignments they have.

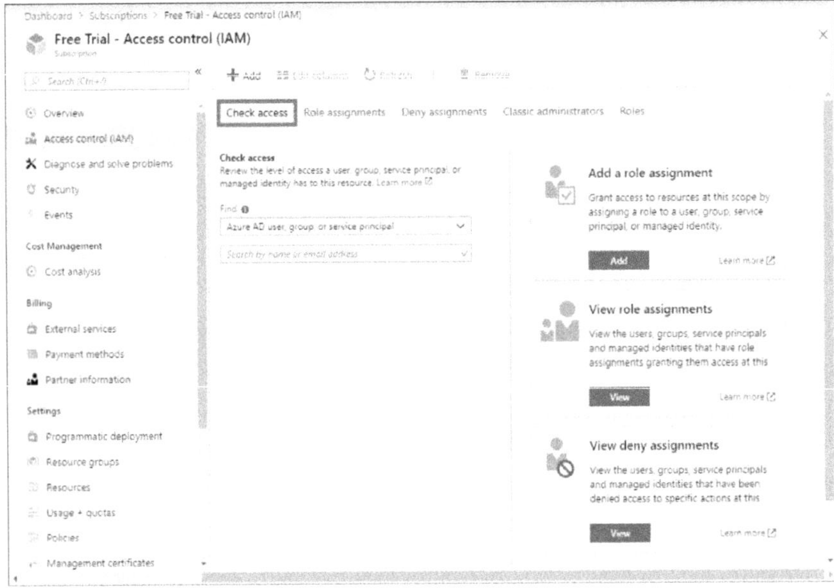

This includes viewing any deny assignments on a given resource or Resource Group in Azure.

Review this website for additional information:

https://docs.microsoft.com/en-us/azure/role-based-access-control/role-assignments-portal#view-role-assignments

Question 37:

A database administrator requires access to all SQL databases in resource groups within your Azure subscription.

You need to maintain security and only grant the access required. What should you do?

1. Grant Owner to the subscription
2. Grant full read/write permissions over the resource groups that have a database within them via Access Control (IAM)
3. Grant full access over the specific databases only using Access Control (IAM)
4. Create a new user for each database with relevant permissions over the database

Explanation

Correct Answer(s): 3

Grant full access over the specific databases only using Access Control (IAM)

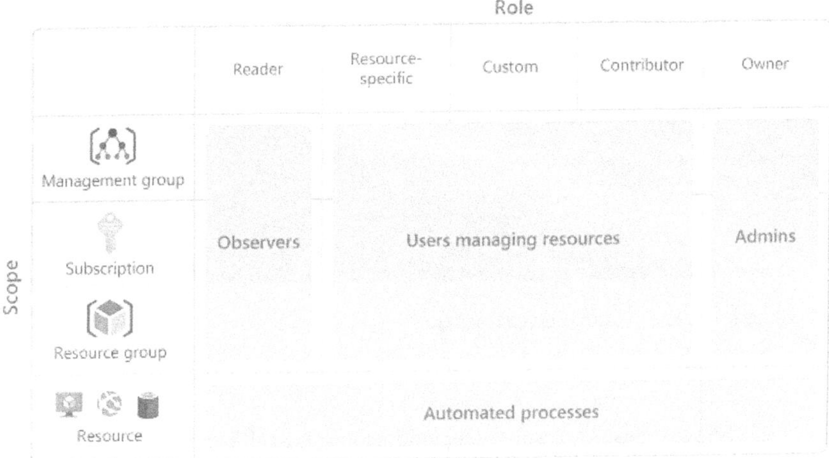

The explanation for the correct answer is:

Although a number of these options would achieve the end goal, RBAC best practices by Microsoft recommend to have the most restrictive permissions. Therefore, giving a DBA full owner permission, or full read/write access over contents of a resource group that they do not need isn't best practice. However, giving access to each individual resource using 'This Resource' as the permission is the best option.

The image shows a recommended pattern for how to use Role-based Access Control.

Review this website for additional information:

https://docs.microsoft.com/en-us/learn/modules/control-and-organize-with-azure-resource-manager/5-role-based-access

Question 38:

You are an IT Manager at Contoso Electronics and are auditing a number of your VMs using Azure Policy.

You run the following command:

Get-AzPolicyState -ResourceGroupName $rg.ResourceGroupName -PolicyAssignmentName 'audit-vm-manageddisks' -Filter 'IsCompliant eq false'

The following is the output from the command:

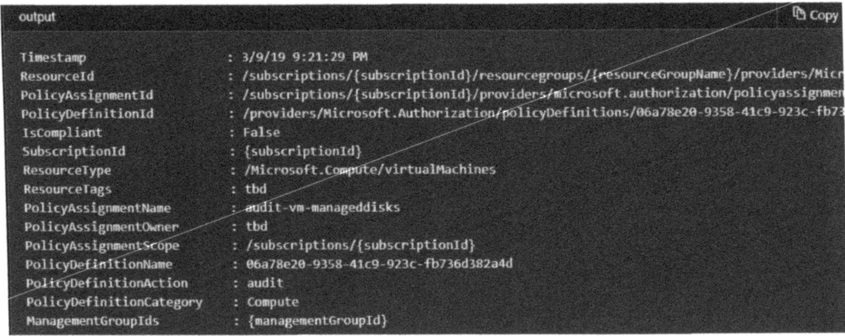

What task has the command performed?

(Choose two.)

1. Shown all resources that are compliant against the audit-vm-manageddisks policy
2. Shown all resources that are not compliant against the audit-vm-manageddisks policy
3. Checked to see if the VM has unmanaged disks attached
4. Checked to see if the VM has more than one Managed Disk

Explanation

Correct Answer(s): 2, 3

Shown all resources that are not compliant against the 'audit-vm-manageddisks' policy

Checked to see if the VM has unmanaged disks attached

The explanation for the correct answer is:

The command is running a specific Azure policy named 'audit-vm-manageddisks' which checks if the VM has any disks that are attached that are not Managed Disks.

The output, which you can see says 'False' next to whether it is compliant, is due to the fact that all VMs should use Managed Disks for security and performance related issues. Running this allows you to ensure your existing infrastructure is compliant against that Azure policy.

The image shows the difference between Azure Policy and RBAC.

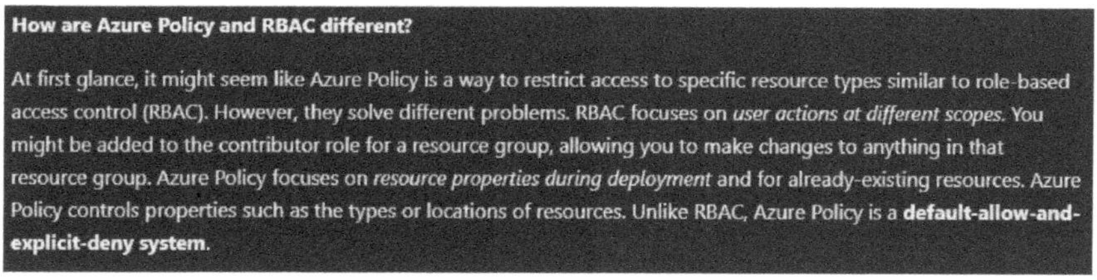

How are Azure Policy and RBAC different?

At first glance, it might seem like Azure Policy is a way to restrict access to specific resource types similar to role-based access control (RBAC). However, they solve different problems. RBAC focuses on *user actions at different scopes*. You might be added to the contributor role for a resource group, allowing you to make changes to anything in that resource group. Azure Policy focuses on *resource properties during deployment* and for already-existing resources. Azure Policy controls properties such as the types or locations of resources. Unlike RBAC, Azure Policy is a **default-allow-and-explicit-deny system.**

Resources:

https://docs.microsoft.com/en-us/learn/modules/intro-to-governance/2-azure-policy

Question 39:

Examine the PowerShell script.

Choose the answer that describes the purpose of the last line of the PowerShell script.

1. Creates a Blob Storage Account container
2. Outputs a list of all of the Blobs in the container
3. Deletes all containers in a blob Storage Account
4. Lists all blobs in a subscription
5. Outputs the Line of Business apps in the container

Explanation

Correct Answer(s): 2

Outputs a list of all of the Blobs in the container

The explanation for the correct answer is:

The PowerShell script outputs a list of all of the Blobs in the container.

The cmdlet Get-AzStorageBlob is used to lists Blobs in a container.

The PowerShell script doesn't create a Blob Storage Account, delete containers or list all Blobs in a subscription.

Review this website for additional information:

https://docs.microsoft.com/en-us/azure/storage/scripts/storage-blobs-container-calculate-size-powershell?toc=%2fpowershell%2fmodule%2ftoc.json

Question 40:

The DevOps Manager has asked you to create Azure Storage Accounts named in the North Europe region.

Your Line of Business App named CycleApp1 is used by all users within your organization.

This storage account will contain CycleApp1 users profile pictures.

CycleApp1 will create thumbnail images for each user, which are 24KB in size. These images will be stored in the CycleSA1 Storage Account.

You also need to create message logs to store the metadata for each thumbnail image.

Which type of Azure Storage Accounts will you use to meet the requirements?

1. Queue Storage
2. Table Storage
3. Blob Storage
4. Azure Files

Explanation

Correct Answer(s): 1, 3

Queue Storage

Blob Storage

The explanation for the correct answer is:

Azure Queue Storage is best suited for the storing and retrieving of messages log information.

Queue messages can be up to 64KB in size.

They will be processed in sequence.

The thumbnail images themselves will be stored using Azure Blob Storage.

Review these websites for additional information:

https://docs.microsoft.com/en-us/azure/storage/common/storage-introduction

https://docs.microsoft.com/en-us/azure/storage/queues/storage-queues-introduction

Question 41:

You are having trouble with Azure File Sync between a Windows 2016 Server.

What troubleshooting steps should you NOT take in trying to resolve this?

1. Choose one or more options that apply.
2. Consult Microsoft Docs troubleshooting pages
3. Remove the Server Endpoint
4. Recreate the Server Endpoint
5. Open an Azure Support ticket with Microsoft

Explanation

Correct Answer(s): 3, 4

Recreate the Server Endpoint

Remove the Server Endpoint

The explanation for the correct answer is:

Removing and/or recreating the Server Endpoint is almost never an appropriate solution to fixing issues with Sync, Cloud Tiering, or other aspects of Azure File Sync, therefore this is incorrect.

Removing a Server Endpoint is a destructive operation and may result in data loss in the case that tiered files exist outside of the Server Endpoint namespace, therefore this is incorrect.

Some of the correct troubleshooting steps include:

Consult Microsoft Docs troubleshooting pages.

Consult the Azure Storage Forum.

Open an Azure Support ticket with Microsoft

Review this website for additional information:

https://docs.microsoft.com/en-us/azure/storage/files/storage-sync-files-troubleshoot?tabs=portal1%2Cazure-portal#im-having-an-issue-with-azure-file-sync-on-my-server-sync-cloud-tiering-etc-should-i-remove-and-recreate-my-server-endpoint

Question 42:

Which option is not a component of the Azure File Sync Agent?

1. FileSyncSvc.exe
2. FilesSyncRegServ.msi
3. StorageSync.sys
4. PowerShell management cmdlets

Explanation

Correct Answer(s): 2

FilesSyncRegServ.msi

The explanation for the correct answer is:

The Azure File Sync Agent is a downloadable package that enables Windows Server to be synced with an Azure file share.

The Azure File Sync Agent has three main components:

FileSyncSvc.exe - this is the background Windows service that is responsible for monitoring changes on server endpoints, and for initiating sync sessions to Azure.

StorageSync.sys - this is the Azure File Sync file system filter, which is responsible for tiering files to Azure Files (when cloud tiering is enabled).

PowerShell management cmdlets - PowerShell cmdlets that you use to interact with the Microsoft.StorageSync Azure resource provider.

FilesSyncRegServ.msi is not a component of the Azure File Sync Agent.

Review this website for additional information:

https://docs.microsoft.com/en-us/azure/storage/files/storage-sync-files-planning#azure-file-sync-agent

Question 43:

To keep files in sync in an Azure File Sync Group you need to define ______?

Choose which answer best completes the sentence.

1. Registered Servers
2. Endpoints
3. Azure File Sync Agents
4. Storage Sync Services

Explanation

Correct Answer(s): 2

Endpoints

The explanation for the correct answer is:

Endpoints within a sync group are kept in sync with each other.

For example, you have two distinct sets of files that you want to manage with Azure File Sync, you would create two sync groups and add different Endpoints to each sync group.

Review this website for additional information:

https://docs.microsoft.com/en-us/azure/storage/files/storage-sync-files-planning#azure-file-sync-terminology

Question 44:

Review the following statement:

An Azure file share can be mounted by Windows, macOS, and/or Linux with the industry standard Server Message Block (SMB) 1.0 protocol or via the File REST API.

Is the statement True or False?

1. FALSE
2. TRUE

Explanation

Correct Answer(s): 1

FALSE

The explanation for the correct answer is:

The answer is False. An Azure File Share can be mounted by Windows, macOS, and/or Linux with the industry standard Server Message Block (SMB) protocol or via the File REST API.

However the only SMB protocols allowed are 2.1 and 3.0.

SMB protocol version 1.0 is not allowed.

Review this website for additional information:

https://docs.microsoft.com/en-us/azure/storage/files/storage-files-planning#data-access-method

Question 45:

You work for CycleShare.com and you have created an Azure File Share called "cyclesh05" with a share called "public" and a directory called "cycleimages'.

Choose the answer that is the correct format for an Azure Files URL.

1. https://cyclesh05.file.core.windows.net/images/cyclepublic
2. https://cyclesh05.file.core.windows.net/public/cycleimages
3. https://cyclesh05.files.share.windows.net/public/cycleimages
4. https://cyclesh05.files.share.windows.net/images/cyclepublic

Explanation

Correct Answer(s): 2

https://cyclesh05.file.core.windows.net/public/cycleimages

The explanation for the correct answer is:

https://cyclesh05.file.core.windows.net/public/cycleimages would be the correct URL format for the Azure File Share.

For requests to an Azure File Share made with the File REST protocol, files are addressable using the following URL format:

https://<storage account>.file.core.windows.net/<share>/<directory>/<file>

https://cyclesh05.file.share.windows.net is incorrect because "files.share" is not a correct URL for Azure File Shares.

Review this website for additional information:

https://docs.microsoft.com/en-us/azure/storage/files/storage-files-planning#management-concepts

Question 46:

The DevOps manager of CycleShare.com asks you setup a Azure File Share for staff to access.

The file share will need to cope with a large amount of data being saved to it.

What is the maximum quota size that an Azure File Share?

1. 5TiB
2. 2TiB
3. 10TiB
4. 520GB

Explanation

Correct Answer(s): 1

5TiB

The explanation for the correct answer is:

The maximum file share size in a Azure File Share is 5TiB

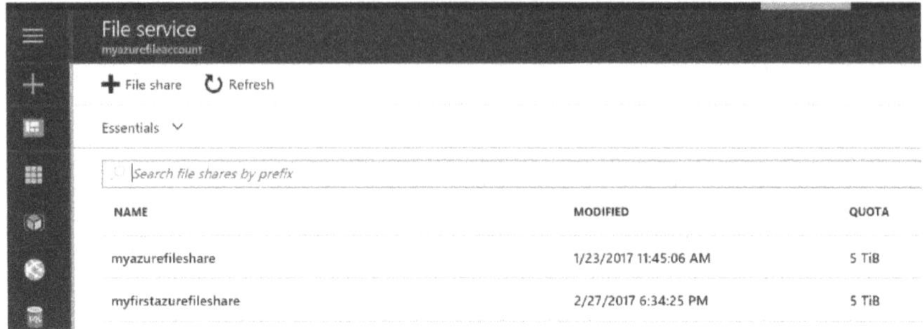

Review this website for additional information:

https://docs.microsoft.com/en-us/azure/storage/files/storage-how-to-create-file-share

Question 47:

You need to create an Azure CDN endpoint.

What protocols are available to select when creating a Azure CDN endpoint?

Choose all that apply.

1. HTTP
2. TLS
3. ICMP
4. CIFS
5. HTTPS

Explanation

Correct Answer(s): 1, 5

HTTP and HTTPS

The explanation for the correct answer is:

HTTP and HTTPs are valid protocols that are available when creating an Azure CDN endpoint.

You can select either HTTP or HTTPS or both.

TLS, ICMP and CIFS are not valid protocols that are available in the creation of Azure CDN endpoints.

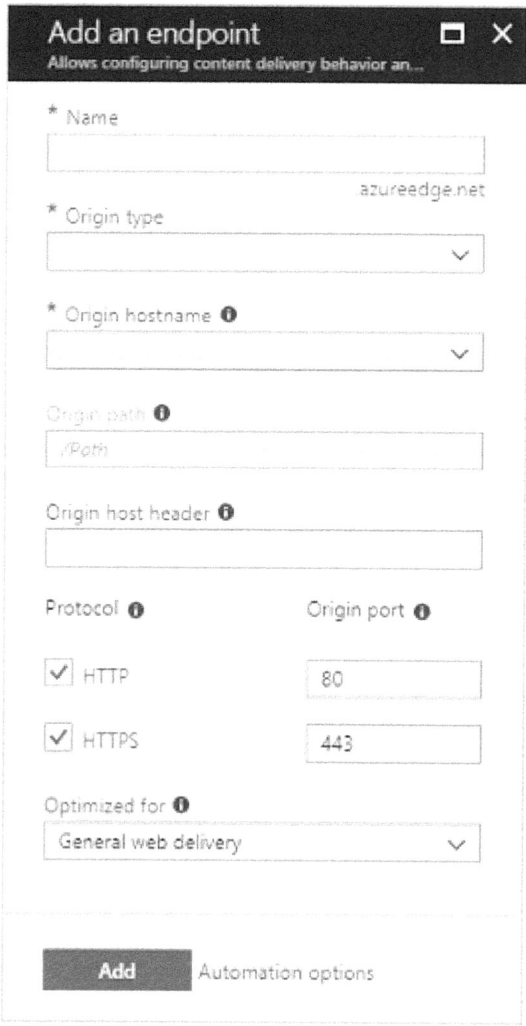

Review this website for additional information:

https://docs.microsoft.com/en-us/azure/cdn/cdn-create-endpoint-how-to

Question 48:

You have been using a Storage Account called cyclestoreapwe1 for application data.

However you believe a an ex-employee may have saved the Shared Key 1 details which allows access to cyclestoreapwe1.

The Security Manager requires that the application data needs to be safeguarded at all times.

How should you secure the application data whilst keeping the application online?

1. Regenerate key 1
2. Regenerate all keys
3. Use key 2 for the application that uses the Storage account and regenerate key 1

Explanation

Correct Answer(s): 3

Use key 2 for the application that uses the Storage account and regenerate key 1

The explanation for the correct answer is:

You should use key 2 for the application that uses the Storage Account and regenerate key 1.

When you create a Storage Account, Azure generates two 512-bit storage account access keys. These keys can be used to authorize access to your Storage Account via Shared Key.

You can rotate and regenerate the keys without interruption to your applications, and Microsoft recommends that you do so regularly.

Review this website for additional information:

https://docs.microsoft.com/en-us/azure/storage/common/storage-account-manage

Question 49:

The DevOps Manager has asked you to create a Azure Storage Account named CycleSA1 in the North Europe region.

Your Line of Business App named CycleApp1 is used by all users within your organization.

CycleApp1 will process thumbnail images for each user, which are 24KB in size. These images will be stored in an Azure Storage Account.

You need also to create message logs to store the metadata for each thumbnail image.

Which type of Azure Storage Account will you use to store message logs?

1. Table Storage
2. Queue Storage
3. Blob Storage
4. Azure Files

Explanation

Correct Answer(s): 2

Queue Storage

The explanation for the correct answer is:

Azure Queue Storage is best suited for the storing and retrieving of messages log information.

Queue messages can be up to 64KB in size.

They will be processed in sequence.

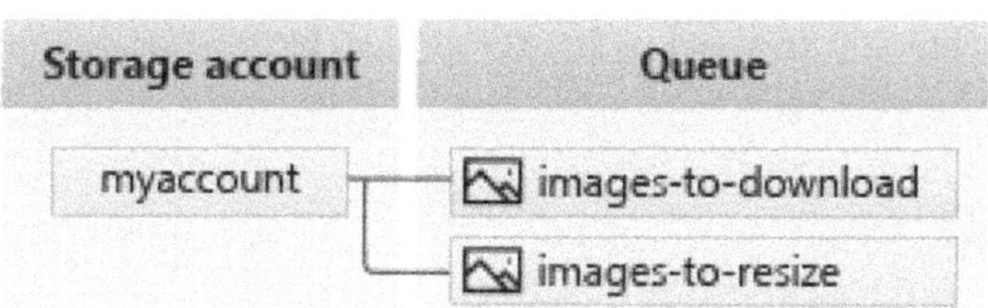

The thumbnail images themselves will be best store using BLOB storage.

Review these websites for additional information:

https://docs.microsoft.com/en-us/azure/storage/common/storage-introduction

https://docs.microsoft.com/en-us/azure/storage/queues/storage-queues-introduction

Question 50:

You are asked to configure an Azure Storage Account that will have a publicly accessible domain name of CycleShare.com.

You need to apply the custom domain name to the Storage Account?

1. Blob Storage
2. Queue Storage
3. Disk Storage
4. Table Storage

Explanation

Correct Answer(s): 1

Blob Storage

The explanation for the correct answer is:

Azure Blob Storage Accounts allow you to use a custom domain name.

You can configure a custom domain for accessing blob data in your Azure Storage Account. The default endpoint for Azure Blob storage is <storage-account-name>.blob.core.windows.net.

If you map a custom domain and subdomain, such as www.cycleshare.com, to the blob or web endpoint for your Storage Account, your users can use that domain to access blob data in your storage account.

Review this website for additional information:

https://docs.microsoft.com/en-us/azure/storage/blobs/storage-custom-domain-name

Question 51:

You have configured a Blob storage account called azsaap01.

Azsaap01 was created as a Standard performance Storage Account using Cool storage on Locally-Redundant Storage (LRS).

Your requirements for azsaap01 have changed since this storage was originally implemented.

Your DevOps manager has advised you that you now need the Storage Account to be amended.

Select which option or options that you can change.

1. Access tier from Cool to Hot
2. Performance from Standard to Premium
3. Blob storage to Table storage

4. Replication from LRS to GRS
5. Change the Resource Group

Explanation

Correct Answer(s): 1, 4, 5

Access tier from Cool to Hot

Replication from LRS to GRS

Change the Resource Group

The explanation for the correct answer is:

Once a Storage Account is created you can amend the following attributes:

Access tier from Cool to Hot

Replication from LRS to GRS

Change the Resource Group

It is not possible to change it from Standard to Premium performance storage or change the type of storage account.

Review this website for additional information:

https://docs.microsoft.com/en-us/azure/storage/blobs/storage-blobs-introduction

Question 52:

You currently manage a Blob Storage Account named CycleBlobSA

CycleBlobSA is currently accessible by all networks.

Your DevOps Manager has asked you to secure CycleBlobSA.

You need to lock CycleBlobSA down to the following IP range:

84.10.200.1 - 84.10.200.254.

How will you configure CycleBlobSA to meet company requirements?

1. In the Firewall and Virtual Networks settings of the Storage Account, select "Selected Networks" and then under Firewall, type the IP address range using CIDR format.

2. Setup a Firewall appliance from the Azure Marketplace. On the Firewall appliance add an allow rule for the IP address range "84.10.200.0/24"
3. In the Firewall and Virtual Networks settings of the Storage Account, select "Selected Networks" and then under Firewall type the IP address "84.10.200.1" and in the next line type "84.10.200.254"
4. In the Firewall and Virtual Networks settings of the Storage Account, select "Selected Networks" and then under Firewall type the IP address range as "84.10.200.1/24"

Explanation

Correct Answer(s): 1

In the Firewall and Virtual Networks settings of the Storage Account, select "Selected Networks" and then under Firewall, type the IP address range using CIDR format.

The explanation for the correct answer is:

You can add the CIDR range directly into the Storage Account settings as "84.10.200.0./24".

The other options are incorrect since they either implement the wrong syntax to add the IP range or they over complicate the configuration.

Setting up a Azure Marketplace appliance can achieve the desired security requirements, but this is not the easiest or most efficient way to achieve the goal.

Review this website for additional information:

https://docs.microsoft.com/en-us/azure/storage/common/storage-network-security

Question 53:

In defining autoscaling rule sets what is the "cooldown" parameter?

1. The amount of time monitored before the metric and threshold values are compared
2. The amount of time to wait before the rule is applied again so that the autoscale actions have time to take effect
3. How often the metrics are collected for analysis
4. Operator used to compare the metric data against the threshold

Explanation

Correct Answer(s): 2

The amount of time to wait before the rule is applied again so that the autoscale actions have time to take effect.

The explanation for the correct answer is:

It is the amount of time to wait before the rule is applied again so that the autoscale actions have time to take effect.

Review this website for additional information:

https://docs.microsoft.com/en-us/azure/virtual-machine-scale-sets/tutorial-autoscale-template

Question 54:

You plan to deploy two new virtual machines.

The virtual machines will be of different sizes.

The VMs will run an application named App2.

You need to ensure that App2 will be tolerant of datacenter failures such as network switch or rack power failure.

What should you create first?

1. An Availability Zone.
2. A Recovery Services Vault.
3. An Availability Set.
4. A Virtual Machine Scale Set.

Explanation

Correct Answer(s): 3

An Availability Set.

The explanation for the correct answer is:

An Availability Set is a logical grouping capability for isolating VM resources from each other when they're deployed to be tolerant of component failures within the datacenter.

VMs cannot be added to Availability Sets after they are deployed, so the availability set must be created first.

A Virtual Machine Scale Set is almost the same, but Scale Set VMs are of the same specification, and the scenario refers to VMs of different sizes.

A Recovery Services Vault could only really be useful if you wanted to replicate a VM into the vault for disaster protection purposes, it would not be suitable to protect two running VMs against Azure fabric failure such as the examples in the question.

Availability Zones are very similar to Availability Sets , but you cannot provision them - they exist already for you to use, and protect against datacenter failure inside a region.

Review this website for additional information:

https://docs.microsoft.com/en-us/azure/virtual-machines/windows/manage-availability#configure-multiple-virtual-machines-in-an-availability-set-for-redundancy

Question 55:

You have deployed a virtual machine named VM4.

VM4 uses the Standard_DS1_v2 size and a managed operating system disk.

You plan to add 6 additional data disks to VM4.

What should you do first?

1. Resize VM4.
2. Redeploy VM4.
3. Create a new general purpose v2 Storage Account.
4. Deallocate VM4.

Explanation

Correct Answer(s): 1

Resize VM4.

The explanation for the correct answer is:

You will need to Resize VM4. The current VM size allows for up to 4 data disks, so to add 6 you will need to change the size of the VM to a SKU that supports 6 or more disks.

Redeploying the VM will not change the size.

Creating a new Storage Account could be a logical step towards getting more disks stored, but without the VM resize it will not achieve the goal.

Deallocating the VM (shutting it down) is not necessary in order to add data disks, but this VM would end up rebooting anyway as part of the resizing process.

Review this website for additional information:

https://docs.microsoft.com/en-us/azure/virtual-machines/windows/sizes-general#dsv2-series

Question 56:

You have a virtual machine named VM1.

You attempt to start VM1 and it fails to start.

You need to recommend a solution that will start VM1 as quickly as possible.

What should you recommend?

1. Deploy VM1 again from a JSON template.
2. Redeploy VM1.
3. Delete VM1, then recreate VM1 using the original operating system disk.
4. Restart VM1.

Explanation

Correct Answer(s): 2

Redeploy VM1.

The explanation for the correct answer is:

You should Redeploy VM1.

If you have been facing difficulties troubleshooting Remote Desktop (RDP) connection or application access to Windows-based Azure virtual machine (VM) you should consider redeploying the VM. When you redeploy a VM, Azure will shut down the VM, move the VM to a new node within the Azure infrastructure, and then power it back on, retaining all your configuration options and associated resources. This takes a very small amount of time, and keeps the VM consistent.

If you were to deploy VM1 again from a JSON template, you would be building a whole new VM which would take more time.

Deleting and recreating the VM from the original operating system disk is similar to deploying the VM.

Restarting VM1 would not resolve the issue, since the VM is not able to be started.

Review this website for additional information:

https://docs.microsoft.com/en-us/azure/virtual-machines/troubleshooting/redeploy-to-new-node-windows

Question 57:

You are tasked with adding Virtual Machines to a resource group called "projectesp01".

You decide to complete this task by creating an Azure Resource Manager template.

The resource group already contains 12 VMs.

You do not want to modify or change the existing VMs.

What deployment method should you use?

1. Complete Mode
2. Update Mode
3. Incremental Mode
4. Additional Mode

Explanation

Correct Answer(s): 3

Incremental Mode

The explanation for the correct answer is:

Incremental Mode is the correct mode.

When using Incremental mode, Azure Resource Manager leaves resources that exist in the resource group unchanged.

Complete Mode is incorrect as this would replace the resources with those specified within the template.

Update Mode and Additional Mode aren't valid modes of deployment for Azure Resource Manager.

Review this website for additional information:

https://docs.microsoft.com/en-us/azure/azure-resource-manager/deployment-modes

Question 58:

What script languages can you run to deploy ARM templates?

Select all that apply.

1. .NET
2. JavaScript
3. C++
4. Pascal
5. Ruby

Explanation

Correct Answer(s): 1, 5

.NET

Ruby

The explanation for the correct answer is:

.NET and Ruby are languages which you can deploy ARM templates from the Azure portal. Other methods to deploy include Azure CLI and PowerShell.

Review this website for additional information:

https://docs.microsoft.com/en-us/azure/azure-resource-manager/resource-manager-quickstart-create-templates-use-the-portal

Question 59:

The DevOps Manager has tasked you with deploying a Linux VM.

You decide to use an ARM template to achieve this.

What value in the JSON template would you use to configure lock down SSH access to the VM?

1. adminPublicKey
2. sshLockdown
3. keySafe
4. variables

Explanation

Correct Answer(s): 1

adminPublicKey

The explanation for the correct answer is:

The adminPublicKey is the correct value to configure locking down SSH.

sshLockdown and keySafe are not valid in ARM templates.

The variables element is not a value itself and would not contain a value to configure this.

Review this website for additional information:

https://docs.microsoft.com/en-us/azure/virtual-machines/linux/create-ssh-secured-vm-from-template

Question 60:

Examine the following PowerShell script:

Get-AzVmssVM -ResourceGroupName "resourcegroup1" -VMScaleSetName "VMSS07"

Select the outcome of running this script.

1. Displays the VM snapshots in a Virtual Machine Scale set named "VMSS07"
2. Configures the VM instances in a Virtual Machine Scale set named "VMSS07"
3. Displays the VM instances in a Virtual Machine Scale set named "VMSS07"
4. Displays the Virtual Managed Disks in the and scale set named "VMSS07"

Explanation

Correct Answer(s): 3

Displays the VM instances in a Virtual Machine Scale set named "VMSS07"

The explanation for the correct answer is:

The Get-AzVmssVM cmdlet gets the model view and instance view of a Virtual Machine Scale Set (VMSS) virtual machine.

The following PowerShell script:

Get-AzVmssVM -ResourceGroupName "resourcegroup1" -VMScaleSetName "VMSS07" gets the properties of the VMSS virtual machine named VMSS07 that belongs to the resource group named resourcegroup1.

Review this website for additional information:

https://docs.microsoft.com/en-us/powershell/module/az.compute/get-azvmssvm?view=azps-1.6.0

Question 61:

What is the maximum number of Virtual machines you can have in a Scale Set?

1. 100
2. 1000
3. 10000
4. 2000

Explanation

Correct Answer(s): 2

1000

The explanation for the correct answer is:

The maximum number of Virtual machines you can have in a Scale Set is 1000.

Review this website for additional information:

https://docs.microsoft.com/en-us/azure/azure-subscription-service-limits#virtual-machine-scale-sets-limits

Question 62:

You are a system administrator at Contoso Electronics looking to migrate from on-premise infrastructure to Azure for your internal website. This is in order to minimise the amount of infrastructure administration and management.

Your current website is a .NET website, hosted on a Windows Server 2016 Server using IIS 8.0. The website has high traffic daily and has a significant number of images and videos, and a high storage requirement of 30GB.

The website requires constant updates.

Choose the most appropriate Azure migration option.

1. A VM with 4GB RAM, 120GB Disk Drive running Windows Server 2016
2. Azure Web Apps on a Free tier App Service Plan
3. Azure Web Apps on a Standard tier App Service Plan
4. Azure Web Apps on a Premium tier App Service Plan

Explanation

Correct Answer(s): 3

Azure Web Apps on a Standard tier App Service Plan

The explanation for the correct answer is:

Although a VM with 4GB RAM, 120GB Disk space and running Windows Server 2016 would be a feasible option, it specifically says that they are trying to minimise the management of the internal infrastructure – so moving to a cloud based VM would not do this.

Azure Web Apps with a Free App Service Plan has a limit of 1GB Disk Space, which would not fulfil the requirements. A Free App Service Plan is also recommended for apps with minimal traffic.

Azure Web Apps with a Standard App Service Plan meets all the requirements, with the exception of needing to clone the app.

Azure Web App with a Premium tier App Service Plan meets all requirements and includes the ability to clone the app.

1. Create a key vault.
2. Set the key vault access policy to support disk encryption.
3. Use the key vault to store the encryption keys for ADE.

Review this website for additional information:

https://azure.microsoft.com/en-us/pricing/details/app-service/plans/

Question 63:

You are the Security and Compliance Officer at Contoso Electronics.

You need to ensure that you are complying to certain regulations and that the data stored on your Azure VMs cannot be accessed by unauthorised users, devices or applications.

Which of the following options should you enable to ensure that all data on your VM disks are encrypted at rest in Azure Storage?

1. Azure Disk Encryption (ADE)
2. Storage Service Encryption (SSE)
3. Encryption on host OS
4. Third Party Encryption

Explanation

Correct Answer(s): 1

Azure Disk Encryption (ADE)

The explanation for the correct answer is:

Azure Disk Encryption (ADE) is managed by the VM Owner, using BitLocker on Windows and DM-Crypt on Linux. These features integrate with the OS and ensures that data at rest is secure by encrypting the data and storing the keys/secrets within Azure Key Vault.

Storage Service Encryption is also used to protect data at rest, by automatically encrypting the data using 256-AES encryption. However, SSE is enabled by default on all new and existing storage accounts and cannot be disabled. SSE does not impact the performance of anything using Azure Storage Services.

Encryption on the host OS is a very manual process that must be remembered to be enabled and often has performance based concerns. There is no integration into Azure.

The image shows the pre-requisites to enable Azure Disk Encryption (ADE)

1. Create a key vault.
2. Set the key vault access policy to support disk encryption.
3. Use the key vault to store the encryption keys for ADE.

Review this website for additional information:

https://docs.microsoft.com/en-us/learn/modules/secure-your-azure-virtual-machine-disks/3-encrypt-existing-vm-disks

Question 64:

You are an IT Manager at Contoso Electronics. You are looking to easily deploy VMs into your existing infrastructure and need to ensure that you always create a 'Standard_A2' VM.

Which of the following parameters would you configure within an Azure Resource Manager template?

1. createOption
2. version
3. virtual machinesize
4. type

Explanation

Correct Answer(s): 3

virtual machinesize

The explanation for the correct answer is:

Within the ARM template, the 'virtual_machinesize' option allows you to specify the type of VM you will create when the script is run.

createOption is used to clarify where the top level parameter gets information, such as using 'fromImage' when specifying where the OSDisk comes from.

Version is used when installing the OS, for instance using 'latest' as the value for version ensures that the latest version of Windows Server is installed.

Type is used to specify which resource you are deploying, for example 'Microsoft.Compute/virutalMachines'

Review this website for additional information:

https://docs.microsoft.com/en-us/learn/modules/choose-compute-provisioning/2-provisioning-solutions

Question 65:

You are looking to deploy a number of VMs and need to create a VHD template.

In order to do this you have to generalize the server.

You have created a backup and are ready to begin. What is your first step?

1. Sign in to the VM, run sysprep.exe, choose Enter system audit mode and Reboot
2. Sign in to the VM, run sysprep.exe, choose Enter System Out-of-Box Experience and Reboot
3. Sign In to the VM, run sysprep.exe, choose Enter system audit mode and shutdown
4. Sign in to the VM, run sysprep.exe, choose Enter System Out-of-Box Experience and Shutdown

Explanation

Correct Answer(s): 4

Sign in to the VM, run sysprep.exe, choose Enter System Out-of-Box Experience and Shutdown

The explanation for the correct answer is:

In order to generalize an image for a template, you need to ensure Sysprep is run using 'Out-of-box Experience (OOBE)'. This essentially resets the system and so you need to ensure that you select Shutdown.

The next step is to deallocate the VM, so having it reboot is the wrong step to move forwards.

Review this website for additional information:

https://docs.microsoft.com/en-us/learn/modules/deploy-vms-from-vhd-templates/3-generalize-server-create-image

Question 66:

Working as the IT Manager at Contoso Electronics you are creating a new scale set and need to ensure that you are able to update the applications installed on the VMs automatically.

You also need to ensure that if there are any update issues you are able to catch the issue prior to it being rolled out to all machines.

Which of the following upgrade policies should you specify when creating your scale set?

1. Manual
2. Rolling
3. Automatic

Explanation

Correct Answer(s): 2

Rolling

The explanation for the correct answer is:

Automatic – This scale set doesn't allow a time for when they are upgraded – meaning they could all updated at the same time. If there any issues this could then cause a service outage.

Rolling – This scale sets performs the update in batches across the VMs specified in your scale set. You can set an optional pause to minimise or eliminate a potential service outage. This does, however, mean that some users may be using different versions of software until they are all updated.

Manual – This is the default option for scale sets. Updates are not completed and all changes must be done manually.

Review this website for additional information:

https://docs.microsoft.com/en-us/learn/modules/build-app-with-scale-sets/6-install-update-applications-virtual-machine-scale-sets

Question 67:

You are a web developer at Contoso Electronics.

You are looking to deploy your website to Azure Web Apps using the default options. Your Web App is called 'ContosoElectronicsWeb'.

Once it is deployed which of the following URLs will be accurate when created?

1. https://ContosoElectronicsWeb.azure-websites.net/
2. http://ContosoElectronicsWeb.azure-websites.co.uk/
3. http://ContosoElectronicsWeb.azurewebsites.net/
4. https://ContosoElectronicsWeb.azurewebsites.net/

Explanation

Correct Answer(s): 3

http://ContosoElectronicsWeb.azurewebsites.net/

The explanation for the correct answer is:

Upon creation, by default you do not have an SSL website using https://. The default domain when creating a web app is 'azurewebsites.net'. Your App Name is unique, so is used to create the first section of your URL.

Review this website for additional information:

https://docs.microsoft.com/en-us/learn/modules/host-a-web-app-with-azure-app-service/3-exercise-create-a-web-app-in-the-azure-portal?pivots=csharp

https://docs.microsoft.com/en-us/learn/modules/app-service-scale-up-scale-out/3-exercise-scale-a-web-app-manually

Question 68:

Listed below are features for one specific Azure offering.

- GPU-Enabled Nodes

- Storage Volume Support

- Identity and Security Management

- Cluster Node Upgrades

- Docker Image Support

- Ingress with HTTP Application Routing SupportWhich service is being described?

1. Azure Kubernetes Service (AKS)
2. Azure Web Apps
3. Azure Container Instances (ACI)
4. Azure Virtual Machine

Explanation

Correct Answer(s): 1

Azure Kubernetes Service (AKS)

The explanation for the correct answer is:

AKS has a number of features that enhance its offering, any of which could be a factor to use AKS.

GPU-Enabled Nodes – AKS Supports GPU enabled node pools, so that if you have any compute-intensive or graphic-intensive workloads, AKS works for you.

Storage Volume Support – AKS offers and supports both static and dynamic storage volumes and can be attached/reattached to storage volumes as they're created.

Identity Security Management – As with other Azure offerings, AKS allows for integration with Azure AD and allows you to use your existing identities and group membership.

Cluster Node Upgrades – AKS gives you the ability of cordoning off nodes and ensuring that during software upgrades, you can minimise disruption to running applications.

Docker Image Support – By default, AKS supports Docker file image format.

Ingress with HTTP Application Routing Support – If your deployed applications need to be available publicly, the HTTP add-on makes this easy with AKS.

Review this website for additional information:

https://docs.microsoft.com/en-us/learn/modules/intro-to-azure-kubernetes-service/4-when-to-use-azure-kubernetes-service

Exam AZ-104 Microsoft Azure Administrator practice exam - Practice Test #2

Question 1:

You are a Database Administrator working for Contoso Electronics.

You are looking to create a service endpoint to ensure that a database is secure, by using a private address space to access the database directly.

Which of the following must be done to enable a service endpoint?

(Select 2)

1. Ensure public access is disabled to the service
2. Ensure public access is enabled to the service
3. Remove the service endpoint from all existing virtual networks
4. Add the service endpoint to an existing virtual network

Explanation

Correct Answer(s): 1, 4

Ensure public access is disabled to the service

Add the service endpoint to an existing virtual network

The explanation for the correct answer is:

When you enable a service endpoint, you restrict the flow of traffic to only devices within your private address space. You are unable to access this service from a public network, such as the internet.

The image shows an example of using a service endpoint, where within Effective routes, the service endpoint is shown as the 'Next Hop Type'.

SOURCE	STATE	ADDRESS PREFIXES	NEXT HOP TYPE
Default	Active	10.1.1.0/24	VNet
Default	Active	0.0.0.0./0	Internet
Default	Active	10.0.0.0/8	None
Default	Active	100.64.0.0./10	None
Default	Active	192.168.0.0/16	None

Review this website for additional information:

https://docs.microsoft.com/en-us/learn/modules/secure-and-isolate-with-nsg-and-service-endpoints/4-vnet-service-endpoints

Question 2:

You are the Cloud Administrator of CycleShare.com a large organisation with multiple sites across the world.

You have created an Azure tenant and want to add your companies domain name CycleShare.com as your primary domain.

Select the options that are required to add this custom domain.

1. Logon to Azure as a Global Administrator.

   Click Azure Active Directory.

   Select Custom domain names, and then select Add custom domain.

   Type in CycleShare.com.

   Copy the DNS TXT record.

   Add this as a DNS TXT record with your domain registrar.

   Click Verify within the custom domains section of Azure.

   Mark the CycleShare.com domain as primary.

2. Logon to Azure as a Global Administrator.

   Click Azure Active Directory.

   Select Custom domain names, and then select Add custom domain.

   Type in CycleShare.com Copy the DNS SRV record.

Add this as a DNS SRV record with your domain registrar. Click Verify within the custom domains section of Azure.

Logon to Azure as a Global Administrator.

Click Azure Active Directory.

3. Select Custom domain names, and then select Add custom domain.

Type in CycleShare.com.

Copy the DNS CSV record.

Add this as a DNS CSV record with your domain registrar.

Click Verify within the custom domains section of Azure.

Mark the CycleShare.com domain as primary.

Logon to Azure as a Global Administrator.

Click Azure Active Directory.

4. Select Custom domain names, and then select Add custom domain.

Type in CycleShare.com.

Click Sync with registrar.

Click Verify within the custom domains section of Azure.

Mark the CycleShare.com domain as primary.

Explanation

Correct Answer(s): 1

Logon to Azure as a Global Administrator.

Click Azure Active Directory.

Select Custom domain names, and then select Add custom domain.

Type in CycleShare.com.

Copy the DNS TXT record.

Add this as a DNS TXT record with your domain registrar.

Click Verify within the custom domains section of Azure.

Mark the CycleShare.com domain as primary.

The explanation for the correct answer is:

You need to copy the given DNS TXT record for your domain to your registrar's DNS, then verify that Azure can see the new DNS TXT record and then finally mark the domain as the primary domain.

Review this website for additional information:

https://docs.microsoft.com/en-gb/azure/active-directory/fundamentals/add-custom-domain

Question 3:

When creating an Azure DNS Zone what two DNS records will be automatically created?

(Select two.)

1. A
2. NS
3. AAAA
4. CNAME
5. SOA

Explanation

Correct Answer(s): 2, 5

NS

SOA

The explanation for the correct answer is:

The following two records are created when creating a DNS Zone.

NS = Name Server record

SOA = Start of Authority

The NS record set at the zone apex (name '@') is created automatically with each DNS zone, and is deleted automatically when the zone is deleted (it cannot be deleted separately).

A SOA record set is created automatically at the apex of each zone (name = '@'), and is deleted automatically when the zone is deleted. SOA records cannot be created or deleted separately.

For more information related to this question, visit:

https://docs.microsoft.com/en-us/azure/dns/dns-zones-records

https://docs.microsoft.com/en-us/azure/dns/private-dns-getstarted-portal

https://docs.microsoft.com/en-us/azure/dns/dns-delegate-domain-azure-dns#create-a-dns-zone

Question 4:

You need to add your companies custom domain CycleShare.com name to Azure Active Directory.

What DNS record(or records do you need to configure to add and verify the domain?

1. A Record - Alias, Destination, TTL & Priority

   TXT Record - Alias, Destination and TTL

2. SRV Record - Alias, Destination, TTL & Priority

   CNAME Record - Destination, TTL

   TXT Record - Alias, Destination and TTL

3. TXT Record - Alias, Destination and TTL
4. MX Record - Alias, Destination, TTL & Priority

Explanation

Correct Answer(s): 3

TXT Record - Alias, Destination and TTL

The explanation for the correct answer is:

The DNS configuration that needs to specified is:

TXT Record - Alias, Destination and TTL

When you configure a custom domain, you will primarily use a TXT Record to validate that you own the domain.

If this is not possible, or if it fails, you will then fall back to set the MX Record.

The correct answer is just the TXT record since this is normally the only record you need to use.

You do not need to configure A, CNAME or SRV records, until after you have validated you have control over the Domain name.

Review this website for additional information:

https://docs.microsoft.com/en-us/azure/active-directory/fundamentals/add-custom-domain

Question 5:

What would be the result of running the following Azure PowerShell cmdlet?

Get-AzExpressRouteServiceProvider

Choose one or more of the options provided.

1. Name
2. PeeringLocations
3. BandwidthsOffered
4. Status

Explanation

Correct Answer(s): 1, 2, 3

Name

PeeringLocations

BandwidthsOffered

The explanation for the correct answer is:

Running the Azure PowerShell cmdlet Get-AzExpressRouteServiceProvider will retrieve the following details for all available providers:

Name

PeeringLocations

BandwidthsOffered

Review this website for additional information:

https://docs.microsoft.com/en-us/azure/expressroute/expressroute-howto-circuit-arm

Question 6:

You will be creating a VPN connection between your Headquarters and the Microsoft Cloud.

You will likely require bandwidth of over 3Gbps and need to ensure the connection is stable and secure, as it will be used for mission-critical workloads.

Which of the following options should you use?

1. Virtual Network, point-to-site
2. Virtual Network, site-to-site
3. ExpressRoute
4. Virtual Network, network-to-network

Explanation

Correct Answer(s): 3

ExpressRoute

The explanation for the correct answer is:

The bandwidth requirement means that only an ExpressRoute VPN would be sufficient in this scenario, as typically a site-to-site bandwidth is < 1Gbps aggregate.

ExpressRoute is also the go-to solution for mission-critical work and enterprise level environments.

The image shows the various benefits of each type of VPN.

Connection	Azure services supported	Bandwidth	Protocols	Typical use case
Virtual network, point-to-site	Azure IaaS services, Azure Virtual Machines	Based on the gateway SKU	Active/passive	Dev, test, and lab environments for cloud services and virtual machines.
Virtual network, site-to-site	Azure IaaS services, Azure Virtual Machines	Typically < 1 Gbps aggregate	Active/passive	Dev, test, and lab environments. Small-scale production workloads and virtual machines.
ExpressRoute	Azure IaaS and PaaS services, Microsoft Office 365 services	50 Mbps up to 10 Gbps (100 Gbps for ExpressRoute Direct)	Active/active	Enterprise-class and mission-critical workloads. Big data solutions.

Review this website for additional information:

https://docs.microsoft.com/en-us/learn/modules/connect-on-premises-network-with-expressroute/4-choose-expressroute

Question 7:

You need to setup a connection to Azure from your on-premises datacenter.

Currently the datacenter hosts your development environment using Azure Stack.

What is the most cost-effective solution that you can implement to connect the on-premises datacenter with the Azure resources?

1. Azure Site-to-Site VPN
2. ExpressRoute
3. Site-to-Site VPN Gateway
4. Web Application Firewall Application Gateway

Explanation

Correct Answer(s): 1

Azure Site-to-Site VPN

The explanation for the correct answer is:

Azure Site-to-Site VPN is the most cost-effective solution for this scenario.

Review this website for additional information:

https://azure.microsoft.com/en-gb/blog/expressroute-or-virtual-network-vpn-whats-right-for-me/

Question 8:

What option best describes the solution that you need to configure to route traffic from your Azure subnet using 10.50.25.0/24 to a virtual firewall appliance?

1. VNet Peering
2. Azure Route Table
3. Virtual Gateway
4. Network Security Gateway

Explanation

Correct Answer(s): 2

Azure Route Table

The explanation for the correct answer is:

The correct answer to meet this requirement is to configure a Azure Route Table.

Review this website for additional information:

https://docs.microsoft.com/en-us/azure/virtual-network/virtual-networks-udr-overview

Question 9:

You need to connect 6 production servers that are located in your Chicago office to your resources in Azure.

Your circuit speed is 100Mbps and you are required to use BGP routing protocol.

What connectivity solution would be the best fit?

1. Site-to-Site VPN Gateway
2. Web Application Firewall Application Gateway
3. ExpressRoute
4. Point-to-Site VPN Gateway

Explanation

Correct Answer(s): 3

ExpressRoute

The explanation for the correct answer is:

ExpressRoute is the only solution which will support the BGP routing protocol.

Review this website for additional information:

https://docs.microsoft.com/en-us/azure/vpn-gateway/vpn-gateway-about-vpngateways

Question 10:

What feature in Azure DNS can translate a IP address to a domain record name?

1. DNS Zone
2. Private DNS
3. An Alias record
4. Reverse DNS

Explanation

Correct Answer(s): 4

Reverse DNS

The explanation for the correct answer is:

Reverse DNS is the feature in Azure DNS can translate a IP address to a domain record name.

For more information related to this question, visit:

https://docs.microsoft.com/en-us/azure/dns/dns-reverse-dns-overview

Question 11:

You need to configure a method of staff connecting remotely to Azure VNets.

Recommend the best method to facilitate this?

1. Point-to-Site VPN
2. ExpressRoute
3. VNet Peering
4. Site-to-Site VPN

Explanation

Correct Answer(s): 1

Point-to-Site VPN

The explanation for the correct answer is:

Point-to-Site VPN is the best method to connect remote users to an Azure VPN. Site-to-Site VPN is to connect other sites together.

ExpressRoute is used to connect large sites directly to Azure, that require large bandwidth capability.

VNet Peering is their to connect VNets inside Azure together.

For more information related to this question, visit:

https://docs.microsoft.com/en-us/azure/vpn-gateway/point-to-site-about

Question 12:

You have created a network security group to apply to the network interface of a new virtual machine. This virtual machine will act as a web server hosted on Azure.

Which of the following default rules are created?

(Select 3)

1. AllowVnetInbound – Priority 65000
2. AllowAzureLoadBalancerInbound – Priority 65001
3. AllowRDPInbound – Priority 65002
4. AllowHTTPInbound – Priority 65003
5. DenyAllInbound – Priority 65500

Explanation

Correct Answer(s): 1, 2 ,5

AllowVnetInbound – Priority 65000

AllowAzureLoadBalancerInbound – Priority 65001

DenyAllInbound – Priority 65500

The explanation for the correct answer is:

The default rules allow inbound and outbound traffic from any VM to another VM within the same subnet. They also allow traffic inbound from the default load balancer to any VM within the subnet.

However, all traffic is denied inbound from an external source. Similarly, all outbound traffic is allowed from the VM to the internet.

The image shows all these rules as well as a description and priority of each.

Priority	Rule name	Description
65000	AllowVnetInbound	Allow inbound coming from any VM to any VM within the subnet.
65001	AllowAzureLoadBalancerInbound	Allow traffic from the default load balancer to any VM within the subnet.
65500	DenyAllInBound	Deny traffic from any external source to any of the VMs.

The default rules for outbound traffic are:

Priority	Rule name	Description
65000	AllowVnetOutbound	Allow outbound going from any VM to any VM within the subnet.
65001	AllowInternetOutbound	Allow outbound traffic going to the internet from any VM.
65500	DenyAllOutBound	Deny traffic from any internal VM to a system outside the virtual network.

Review this website for additional information:

https://docs.microsoft.com/en-us/learn/modules/secure-and-isolate-with-nsg-and-service-endpoints/2-network-security-groups

Question 13:

You need to configure a Site-to-Site VPN between an on-premises environment and Azure.

What do you require to configure the on-premises VPN element?

1. Private IP Address of the Virtual Network Gateway and Azure Subscription name
2. Public IP Address of the Virtual Network Gateway, the BGP ASN and a Shared Key
3. Public IP Address of the Virtual Network Gateway and a Shared Key
4. Public IP Address of the Virtual Network Gateway and the BGP ASN

Explanation

Correct Answer(s): 3

Public IP Address of the Virtual Network Gateway and a Shared Key

The explanation for the correct answer is:

The configure the on-premises VPN to establish a connection you require:

Public IP Address of the Virtual Network Gateway and a Shared Key

You do not need the subscription name and it is not a requirement to configure BGP.

Review this website for additional information:

https://docs.microsoft.com/en-us/azure/vpn-gateway/vpn-gateway-howto-site-to-site-resource-manager-portal#VPNDevice

Question 14:

How many Azure Network Watcher packet captures can you run for Azure VMs located in the East US region?

1. 20
2. 10,000
3. 5
4. 100
5. 10

Explanation

Correct Answer(s): 2

10,000

The explanation for the correct answer is:

The maximum Network Watcher Packet Capture sessions per region is 10,000.

Previously the limit was 100, but this has been increased to 10,000 as per the current Microsoft documentation below.

Default (and maximum) packet capture sessions = 10,000. Number of sessions only, not saved captures.

Network Watcher limits

Resource	Default limit	Maximum limit	Note
Azure Network Watcher	1 per region	1 per region	Network Watcher is created to enable access to the service. Only one instance of Network Watcher is required per subscription per region.
Packet capture sessions	10,000 per region	10,000	Number of sessions only, not saved captures.

Review this website for additional information:

https://docs.microsoft.com/en-us/azure/azure-subscription-service-limits#network-watcher-limits

Question 15:

You need to capture packets to diagnose a networking issue on an Azure Windows Server 2019 Virtual Machine.

What should you configure to help diagnose the issue?

(Select one or more tools.)

1. Enable Network Watcher region
2. Azure Network Watcher Agent
3. Network Security Group Flow logging
4. WireShark
5. Microsoft Network Message Analyzer

Explanation

Correct Answer(s): 1, 2

Enable Network Watcher region

Azure Network Watcher Agent

The explanation for the correct answer is:

You need to configure the following to be capture packets with Network Watcher: Enable Network Watcher region

Azure Network Watcher Agent

Review this website for additional information:

https://docs.microsoft.com/en-us/azure/virtual-machines/extensions/network-watcher-windows

Question 16:

What Azure Network Watcher PowerShell cmdlet will allow you see if there are any latency issues in an Azure region?

1. Get-AzNetworkWatcherReachabilityReport
2. Get-AzNetworkWatcherReachabilityProvidersList
3. Get-AzEffectiveNetworkSecurityGroup
4. Test-AzNetworkWatcherIPFlow

Explanation

Correct Answer(s): 1

Get-AzNetworkWatcherReachabilityReport

The explanation for the correct answer is:

Get-AzNetworkWatcherReachabilityReport is the best cmdlet to run to determine latencies in an Azure region.

Get-AzNetworkWatcherReachabilityProvidersList returns providers list to help determine the relative latencies to all Azure regions from a specific physical location provider. This can help you pinpoint an issue with a provider.

Get-AzEffectiveNetworkSecurityGroup to review the effective security rules for the network interface.

Test-AzNetworkWatcherIPFlow tests traffic flow between devices.

For more information related to this question, visit:

https://docs.microsoft.com/en-us/azure/network-watcher/view-relative-latencies

Question 17:

You want to use Azure Network Watcher to troubleshoot routing issues inside your Azure environment.

What feature of Network Watcher should you use?

1. Next Hop

2. IP Flow Verify
3. Security Group View
4. Network Subscription limit

Explanation

Correct Answer(s): 1

Next Hop

The explanation for the correct answer is:

Next Hop would be the best tool to help you diagnose routing problems.

IP Flow Verify is a tool for diagnosing traffic flowing and whether any NSG or devices are blocking that traffic.

Security Group View gives you a graphical network representation.

Network Subscription limit gives you metrics on the subscriptions network.

For more information related to this question, visit:

https://docs.microsoft.com/en-us/azure/network-watcher/network-watcher-next-hop-overview

Question 18:

You are considering deploying an Azure Load Balancer.

Which of the following features is not supported by an Azure Load Balancer?

1. SSL Offload (sometimes known as TLS termination).
2. HTTP Health Probes.
3. Inbound NAT Rules.
4. IPv6 Load Balancing Rules.

Explanation

Correct Answer(s): 1

SSL Offload (sometimes known as TLS termination).

The explanation for the correct answer is:

The Azure Load Balancer does not support SSL/TLS Offload, meaning that any encrypted traffic is simply forwarded to the endpoints in the backend pool without any encryption stripped off first.

In Azure you would use Application Gateway instead of an Azure Load Balancer to meet this requirement.

All other features are supported by the Azure Load Balancer.

Review this website for additional information:

https://docs.microsoft.com/en-us/azure/load-balancer/load-balancer-overview#why-use-load-balancer

Question 19:

What is the limitation on a public facing Azure Load Balancers backend pool Virtual Machines?

1. They must belong to an Availability Set.
2. They must belong to the same single Virtual Network.
3. They must all be allocated.
4. They must be of the same size.

Explanation

Correct Answer(s): 2

They must belong to the same single Virtual Network.

The explanation for the correct answer is:

Backend pools can contain a number of single Virtual Machines (or Scale Sets or Availability Sets), but they must belong to the same Virtual Network.

Review this website for additional information:

https://docs.microsoft.com/en-us/azure/load-balancer/load-balancer-overview#skus

Question 20:

You plan to deploy 3 Virtual Machines (VMs) that will run a web application named Webapp1.

Webapp1 must be made highly available in case one or more of the virtual machines fails.

What should you create to ensure that users can always access Webapp1?

1. An Azure Load Balancer that contains three backend pools and one load balancing rule.
2. An Azure Load Balancer that contains one backend pool and one load balancing rule.
3. An Azure Load Balancer that contains one backend pool and three load balancing rules.
4. An Azure Load Balancer that contains three backend pools and three load balancing rules.

Explanation

Correct Answer(s): 2

An Azure Load Balancer that contains one backend pool and one load balancing rule.

The explanation for the correct answer is:

You need an Azure Load Balancer that contains one backend pool and one load balancing rule that balances traffic such as HTTP on port 80 to the backend pool.

Review this website for additional information:

https://docs.microsoft.com/en-us/azure/load-balancer/load-balancer-overview

Question 21:

You are configuring an Azure Load Balancer.

You need to identify what can be added in a backend pool instance.

What should you identify?

1. Availability Sets, Virtual Machine Scale Sets and single Virtual Machines.
2. Virtual Machine Scale Sets, single Virtual Machines and IPv4 addresses.
3. Single Virtual Machines and IPv4 addresses.
4. Availability Sets and single Virtual Machines.

Explanation

Correct Answer(s): 1

Availability Sets, Virtual Machine Scale Sets and single Virtual Machines.

The explanation for the correct answer is:

Backend pools are the targets for the Azure Load Balancer and can be used with:

Availability Sets, Virtual Machine Scale Sets and single Virtual Machines.

Review this website for additional information:

https://docs.microsoft.com/en-us/azure/load-balancer/load-balancer-overview

Question 22:

You work for CycleShare.com as the Cloud Administrator.

A member of staff asks you to investigate a potential issue with communication with a VM named WebApp1.

WebApp1 has a NIC named WebApp1Nic.

You need to troubleshoot the VM.

What cmdlet will list the effective security rules in place?

1. Get-AzEffectiveNetworkSecurityGroup -NetworkInterfaceName WebApp1Nic -ResourceGroupName myRGweb2
2. Diag-AzNetworkSecurityGroupRules -NetworkInterfaceName WebApp1Nic -ResourceGroupName myRGweb2
3. Get-AzEffectiveNetworkInterfaceRules -NetworkInterfaceName WebApp1Nic -ResourceGroupName myRGweb2
4. Get-AzEffectiveNetworkSecurityGroup -NetworkInterfaceName WebApp1 -ResourceGroupName myRGweb2

Explanation

Correct Answer(s): 1

Get-AzEffectiveNetworkSecurityGroup -NetworkInterfaceName WebApp1Nic -ResourceGroupName myRGweb2

The explanation for the correct answer is:

The correct cmdlet to use is:

Get-AzEffectiveNetworkSecurityGroup -NetworkInterfaceName WebApp1Nic -ResourceGroupName myRGweb2

This retrieves the effective security rules in place for a network interface.

Review this website for additional information:

https://docs.microsoft.com/en-us/azure/virtual-network/diagnose-network-traffic-filter-problem#diagnose-using-powershell

Question 23:

You need to configure a Network Security Group rule to allow RDP access to an Windows Virtual Machine in Azure.

What default port will you need to specify?

1. TCP 3398
2. UDP 3398
3. TCP 3389
4. UDP 3389

Explanation

Correct Answer(s): 3

TCP 3389

The explanation for the correct answer is:

The correct port to allow access to a Windows Virtual Machine in Azure via RDP is TCP 3389.

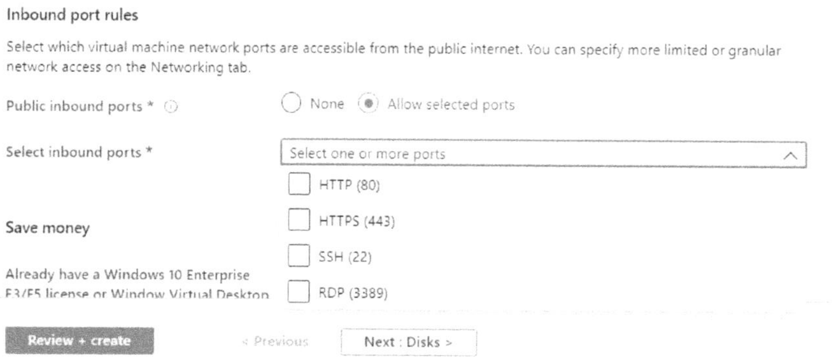

Inbound port rules

Select which virtual machine network ports are accessible from the public internet. You can specify more limited or granular network access on the Networking tab.

Public inbound ports * ⓘ ◯ None ◉ Allow selected ports

Select inbound ports * Select one or more ports

☐ HTTP (80)

Save money ☐ HTTPS (443)

☐ SSH (22)

Already have a Windows 10 Enterprise E3/E5 license or Window Virtual Desktop ☐ RDP (3389)

Review + create < Previous Next : Disks >

Review this website for additional information:

https://docs.microsoft.com/en-us/azure/virtual-machines/troubleshooting/troubleshoot-rdp-nsg-problem

Question 24:

Which is the correct Azure CLI cmdlet to create a Network Security Group (NSG)?

1. az sec nsg update
2. az nsg create
3. az network nsg create
4. az security nsg create

Explanation

Correct Answer(s): 3

az network nsg create

The explanation for the correct answer is:

The correct cmdlet to create an NSG from the Azure CLI is:

az network nsg create

Review this website for additional information:

https://docs.microsoft.com/en-us/cli/azure/network/nsg?view=azure-cli-latest#az-network-nsg-create

Question 25:

Examine the following statement regarding Network Security Groups rules.

Rules are processed in priority order, with higher numbers processed before lower numbers. Once traffic matches a rule, processing stops. As a result, any rules that exist with lower priorities (lower numbers) that have the same attributes as rules with higher priorities are not processed.

Is the statement is True or False?

1. TRUE
2. FALSE

Explanation

Correct Answer(s): 2

FALSE

The explanation for the correct answer is:

The statement is False.

Rules are processed in priority order, with lower numbers processed before higher numbers, because lower numbers have higher priority.

Once traffic matches a rule, processing stops.

As a result, any rules that exist with lower priorities (higher numbers) that have the same attributes as rules with higher priorities are not processed.

Review this website for additional information:

https://docs.microsoft.com/en-us/azure/virtual-network/security-overview#security-rules

Question 26:

You receive reports from other administrators that they are finding it difficult to understand and modify new Network Security Group Rules between two Virtual Networks.

How can you simplify this situation for the Administrators in your organization?

1. Implement Augmented Security Rules

2. Introduce Simple Security Rules
3. Implement Bounded Security Rules
4. Introduce a new Virtual Firewall Appliance from the Azure Marketplace

Explanation

Correct Answer(s): 1

Implement Augmented Security Rules

The explanation for the correct answer is:

Augmented Security Rules can simplify security definition for virtual networks, allowing you to define larger and complex network security policies, with fewer rules. In this way, you can combine multiple ports and multiple explicit IP addresses and ranges into a single, easily understood security rule.

Introducing a Virtual Firewall Appliance wouldn't ensure the rule base is simpler to understand.

Bounded Security Rules and Simple Security Rules are not valid Azure NSG features.

Review this website for additional information:

https://docs.microsoft.com/en-us/azure/virtual-network/security-overview#augmented-security-rules

Question 27:

Examine the following PowerShell cmdlet and choose the answer that best describes its intended usage.

1. New-AzDnsRecordSet
2. Creates one or more DNS record(s)
3. Creates a new DNS zone
4. Creates multiple DNS records
5. Lists all DNS records in a zone

Explanation

Correct Answer(s): 2

Creates one or more DNS record(s)

The explanation for the correct answer is:

The PowerShell cmdlet New-AzDnsRecordSet can create a single or multiple DNS record(s) within a RecordSet.

It does not create a new DNS zone, list all zone records or create multiple DNS records.

Example: You create record sets by using the New-AzDnsRecordSet cmdlet. The following example creates a record with the relative name "www" in the DNS Zone "contoso.xyz", in resource group "MyResourceGroup". The fully qualified name of the record set is "www.contoso.xyz". The record type is "A", with IP address "10.10.10.10", and the TTL is 3600 seconds.

New-AzDnsRecordSet -Name www -RecordType A -ZoneName contoso.xyz -ResourceGroupName MyResourceGroup -Ttl 3600 -DnsRecords (New-AzDnsRecordConfig -IPv4Address "10.10.10.10")

Review this website for additional information:

https://docs.microsoft.com/en-us/azure/dns/dns-getstarted-powershell

Question 28:

The DevOps Manager wants to use DNS for name resolution across your Azure estate.

This includes several VNets across two Azure regions.

You need to ensure that addresses are only resolvable for your resources and not across the internet.

What solution will satisfy your requirements?

1. Reverse DNS
2. DNS with Traffic Manager
3. Private DNS
4. Public DNS

Explanation

Correct Answer(s): 3

Private DNS

The explanation for the correct answer is:

Private DNS is the Azure DNS solution that will best suit the requirements.

Private DNS offers the following characteristics:

Used across up to 1000 VNets across multiple regions.

Name resolution cannot work over the internet.

Review this website for additional information:

https://docs.microsoft.com/en-us/azure/dns/dns-faq-private

Question 29:

Review the following statement:

Azure DNS supports zone transfers

Is the statement True or False?

1. TRUE
2. FALSE

Explanation

Correct Answer(s): 2

FALSE

The explanation for the correct answer is:

FALSE - Azure DNS does not currently support zone transfers.

DNS zones can be imported into Azure DNS by using the CLI.

For more information related to this question, visit:

https://docs.microsoft.com/en-us/azure/dns/dns-faq#does-azure-dns-support-zone-transfers-axfrixfr

Question 30:

Which of the following IT ranges cannot be configured as a valid IP address range in VNets?

1. 224.0.0.0/4
2. 127.0.0.0/8

3. 168.63.129.16/32
4. 10.2.0.0/16
5. 169.254.0.0/16
6. 255.255.255.255/32

Explanation

Correct Answer(s): 1, 2 3, 5, 6

224.0.0.0/4 (Multicast)

255.255.255.255/32 (Broadcast)

127.0.0.0/8 (Loopback)

169.254.0.0/16 (Link-local)

168.63.129.16/32 (Internal DNS)

The explanation for the correct answer is:

The following are not valid IP subnet address ranges that you can use with VNets:

224.0.0.0/4 (Multicast)

255.255.255.255/32 (Broadcast)

127.0.0.0/8 (Loopback)

169.254.0.0/16 (Link-local)

168.63.129.16/32 (Internal DNS)

10.2.0.0/16 is a valid address range to use in a VNet.

The address ranges enumerated in RFC 1918, cannot be used in Azure:

224.0.0.0/4 (Multicast)

255.255.255.255/32 (Broadcast)

127.0.0.0/8 (Loopback)

169.254.0.0/16 (Link-local)

168.63.129.16/32 (Internal DNS)

For more information related to this question, visit:

https://docs.microsoft.com/en-us/azure/virtual-network/virtual-network-ip-addresses-overview-arm#private-ip-addresses

https://docs.microsoft.com/en-us/azure/virtual-network/virtual-networks-faq

Question 31:

You are a Web Developer for Contoso Electronics and are creating a load balancer within Azure.

You need to ensure that a user's session is maintained.

Keeping this in mind, which of the following distribution modes should you use?

1. Source IP Affinity
2. Five-Tuple Hash

Explanation

Correct Answer(s): 1

Source IP Affinity

The explanation for the correct answer is:

In order to maintain the user's session you must use sourceIP affinity. Because the client will always be directed to the same server the profile is stored on that machine maintaining the user session. When you create the load balancer endpoint, sourceIP must be used when you set the distribution.

The image shows how you would set this within the Azure Portal, where you set 'Session persistence' to 'Client IP'.

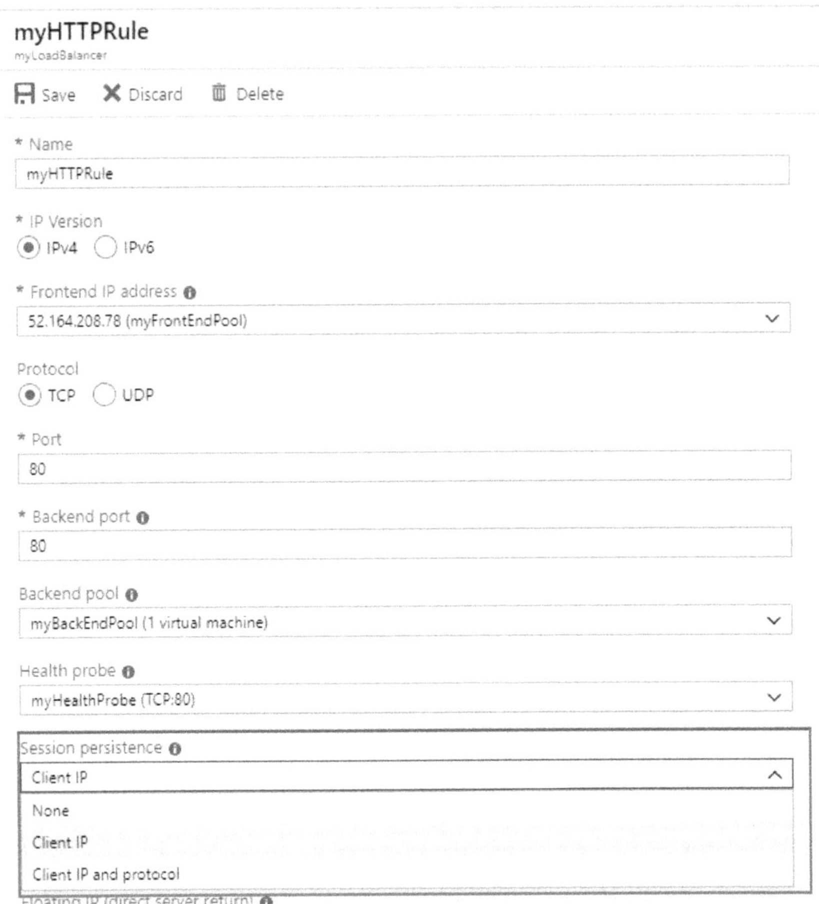

Review this website for additional information:

https://docs.microsoft.com/en-us/learn/modules/improve-app-scalability-resiliency-with-load-balancer/3-public-load-balancer

Question 32:

You need to add a route to an Azure Route Table.

Select the possible Next Hop Types that are available.

(Select all that apply.)

1. Virtual Appliance
2. Internet
3. Network Security Gateway

4. Load Balancer
5. Virtual Network Gateway
6. Storage Account

Explanation

Correct Answer(s): 1, 2, 5

Virtual Network Gateway

Internet

Virtual Appliance

The explanation for the correct answer is:

The following are valid Next Hop Types: Virtual Network Gateway

Virtual Network

Internet

Virtual Appliance

Review this website for additional information:

https://docs.microsoft.com/en-us/azure/virtual-network/virtual-networks-udr-overview

Question 33:

You are looking to create a VPN from your on-premises infrastructure to Azure.

However, you also want to ensure you can have a VPN to other Microsoft cloud services like Office 365 and Dynamics 365, maintaining that security.

Which service should you use?

1. Point-to-Point VPN
2. Network-to-Network VPN
3. Site-to-Site VPN
4. ExpressRoute

Explanation

Correct Answer(s): 4

ExpressRoute

The explanation for the correct answer is:

ExpressRoute allows you to seamlessly extend your on-premises network into various Microsoft cloud services. This connection between Azure and your own infrastructure is dedicated and private, meaning that security is still maintained.

There are a number of benefits to using ExpressRoute, such as Layer 3 Connectivity, Built-in Redundancy as well as the already mentioned connectivity to other Microsoft cloud services.

The image shows an example where ExpressRoute is used.

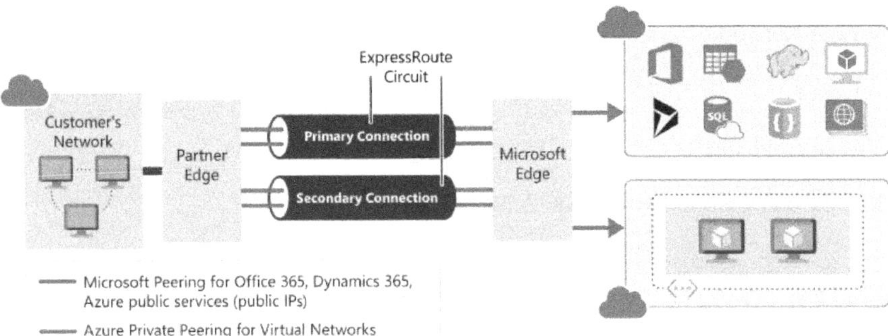

Review this website for additional information:

https://docs.microsoft.com/en-us/learn/modules/connect-on-premises-network-with-expressroute/2-expressroute-service

Question 34:

You are configuring Public IP Addresses for Virtual Machines which are configured as availability sets.

The Virtual Machines disks need to be redundant over different zones but in the same Azure region.

What solution best meets this requirement?

1. A Enterprise SKU Public IP Address needs to be configured
2. A Standard SKU Public IP Address needs to be configured

3. A Free SKU Public IP Address needs to be configured
4. A Basic SKU Public IP Address needs to be configured

Explanation

Correct Answer(s): 2

A Standard SKU Public IP Address needs to be configured

The explanation for the correct answer is:

A Standard SKU Public IP Address needs to be configured to enable zone redundancy as the basic SKU does not support this.

Enterprise and Free Public IP SKUs do not exist in Azure.

Review this website for additional information:

https://docs.microsoft.com/en-us/azure/virtual-network/virtual-network-ip-addresses-overview-arm

Question 35:

Which of the following features are required prior to being able to deploy an operational Azure VPN Gateway?

(Select 6)

1. Virtual Machine
2. Virtual Network
3. GatewaySubnet
4. Public IP Address
5. Local Network Gateway
6. Virtual Network Gateway
7. Connection

Explanation

Correct Answer(s): 2, 3, 4, 5, 6, 7

Virtual Network

GatewaySubnet

Public IP Address

Local Network Gateway

Virtual Network Gateway

Connection

The explanation for the correct answer is:

Virtual Network – When you create a virtual network ensure that you have enough space for the additional subnet that will be used for the VPN Gateway. The address space must not overlap with the on-premises network to which you will be connecting. You can only deploy a single VP Gateway within a virtual network.

Gateway Subnet – You must use at least a /27 address mask to ensure you have enough IP Addresses in the subnet for future growth. You cannot use this subnet for any other services.

Public IP Address – This address is used as a publicly-routable IP and is the target for your on-premises VPN Device. Whilst this IP is dynamic it will not change unless you delete and recreate the VPN Gateway.

Local Network Gateway – Create a LNG to define the on-premises networks configuration, where the VPN gateway will connect as well as to where it will connect.

Virtual Network Gateway – Create the Virtual Network Gateway to route the traffic between your destinations.

Connection – Create the connection itself between your VPN Gateway and the Local Network Gateway. Note you are able to create more than one connection if required.

The image gives an example of how each of the noted features are used to create an operational VPN Gateway.

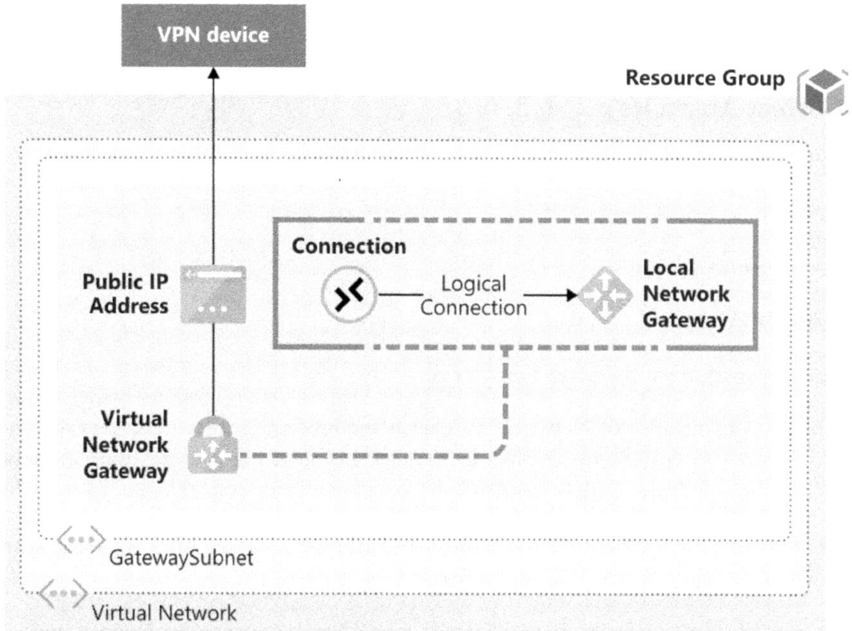

Review this website for additional information:

https://docs.microsoft.com/en-us/learn/modules/connect-on-premises-network-with-vpn-gateway/2-connect-on-premises-networks-to-azure-using-site-to-site-vpn-gateways

Question 36:

You will be using Azure Network Watcher to check usage and quota on certain metrics.

Which of the following metrics are collected when using Network Watcher?

(Select 4)

1. Subnets
2. Network Interfaces
3. VPN Gateways
4. Network Security Groups (NSGs)
5. Virtual Networks
6. Public IP Address
7. Virtual Network Gateways

Explanation

Correct Answer(s): 2, 4, 5, 6

Network Interfaces

Network Security Groups (NSGs)

Virtual Networks

Public IP Address

The explanation for the correct answer is:

One a single instance of Network Watcher is required per subscription, per region. This is used to ensure you are able to monitor if you are at risk of hitting a quota on a specific resource within Azure.

In order to view the metrics, you would go to the Networking blade within Azure > Network Watcher > Usage and quotas.

The image shows an example of what is shown when looking in the Azure portal.

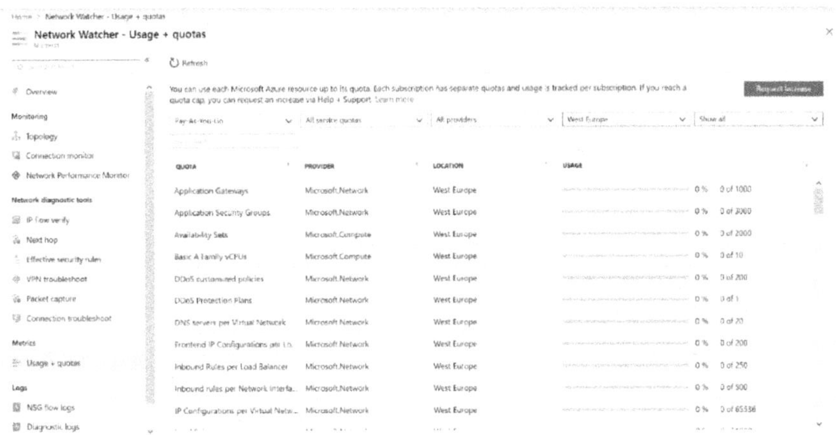

Review this website for additional information:

https://docs.microsoft.com/en-us/learn/modules/troubleshoot-azure-network-infrastructure/4-troubleshoot-networking-with-network-watcher-metrics-logs

Question 37:

CycleShare.com maintains two networks in Azure:

10.20.0.0/16

10.100.26.0/24

Choose one or more valid Azure Private IP addresses that fall within the CycleShare.com networks.

1. 10.100.0.3
2. 10.20.0.50
3. 10.100.26.242
4. 10.100.0.255
5. 10.20.0.2

Explanation

Correct Answer(s): 2, 3

10.20.0.50

10.100.26.242

The explanation for the correct answer is:

The valid IP addresses are 10.20.0.50 and 10.100.26.242

10.20.0.2 and 10.100.0.3 can not be used as these are reserved.

Note: The first four IP address (10.20.0.0-10.20.0.3) within a private address range are reserved and cannot be assigned to resources.

10.100.0.255 in a CIDR/24 network would be used as the broadcast address and cannot be assigned to resources.

Review this website for additional information:

https://docs.microsoft.com/en-us/azure/virtual-network/virtual-network-ip-addresses-overview-arm#private-ip-addresses

Question 38:

You are an IT Manager at Contoso Electronics.

You have applied a Network Security Group to both the subnet and the network interface within your Virtual Network.

In which order is traffic first evaluated when coming in and out of the network?

1. Inbound: Subnet / Network Interface – Outbound: Network Interface / Subnet
2. Inbound: Network Interface / Subnet – Outbound: Subnet / Network Interface
3. Outbound: Network Interface / Subnet – Inbound: Subnet / Network Interface
4. Inbound: Subnet / Network Interface – Outbound: Network Interface / Subnet
5. Inbound: Network Interface / Subnet – Outbound: Network Interface / Subnet
6. Inbound: Subnet / Network Interface – Outbound: Subnet / Network Interface

Explanation

Correct Answer(s): 1

Inbound: Subnet / Network Interface – Outbound: Network Interface / Subnet

The explanation for the correct answer is:

Inbound traffic always passed via the subnet NSG and then by the network interface NSG. Vice versa, outbound traffic is always scanned by the network interface NSG first followed by the subnet NSG. The image shows an example.

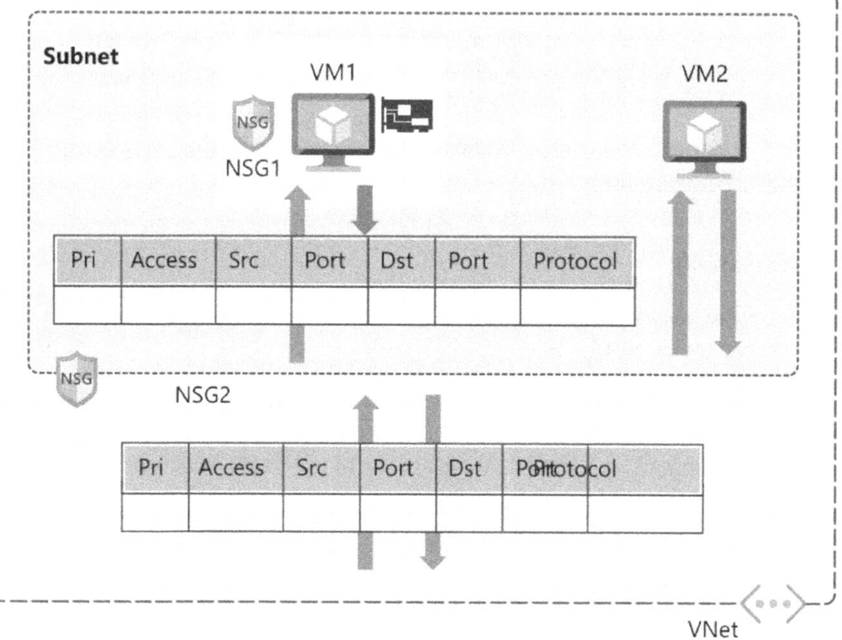

Review this website for additional information:

https://docs.microsoft.com/en-us/learn/modules/secure-and-isolate-with-nsg-and-service-endpoints/2-network-security-groups

Question 39:

Which of the following options would be most suitable for deploying a Standard SKU Public IP address?

1. Basic Back-end Load Balancer
2. Standard Internet-facing Load Balancer
3. Standard Back-end Load Balancer
4. Basic Internet-facing Load Balancer

Explanation

Correct Answer(s): 2

Standard Internet-facing Load Balancer

The explanation for the correct answer is:

A Standard Internet-facing Load-balancer (Standard public Load Balancer) is the only option that would work with an Azure Standard SKU Public IP address.

Review this website for additional information:

https://docs.microsoft.com/en-us/azure/virtual-network/virtual-network-ip-addresses-overview-arm

Question 40:

You need to ensure that Production SQL servers in Subnet1 cannot talk to DMZ Web Servers in Subnet2.

What is the most cost effective solution to meet this requirement?

1. Configure an Firewall Appliance to block traffic between Subnet1 and Subnet2
2. Configure NSGs to block traffic between Subnet1 and Subnet2
3. Configure Route Tables on each VM to block traffic between Subnet1 and Subnet2
4. Configure an Application Gateway to block traffic between Subnet1 and Subnet2

Explanation

Correct Answer(s): 2

Configure NSGs to block traffic between Subnet1 and Subnet2

The explanation for the correct answer is:

Configuring NSGs to block traffic between Subnet1 and Subnet2 is the correct solution.

An Application Gateway will not block traffic.

A Firewall Appliance would be effective, but this would be more costly.

Route Tables would be hard to maintain and therefore not appropriate for this scenario.

Review this website for additional information:

https://docs.microsoft.com/en-us/azure/virtual-network/security-overview

Question 41:

You plan on using Application Gateway to forward traffic to the relevant servers in your Azure Virtual Network.

What does Application Gateway use to forward traffic?

1. Hostname, port and path in the URL
2. Source IP address
3. Geographic location closest to the client

Explanation

Correct Answer(s): 1

Hostname, port and path in the URL

The explanation for the correct answer is:

Application Gateway routes traffic to a pool of web servers based on the URL. This is known as application layer routing. It's important to note that this pool can be anything from Azure VMs, scale sets, app services or even on-premises servers.

There are multiple types of routing, such as path-based routing. For instance, you could direct http://url.com/images to specific image servers and http://url.com/video to another pool of video servers. The image shows how this can work.

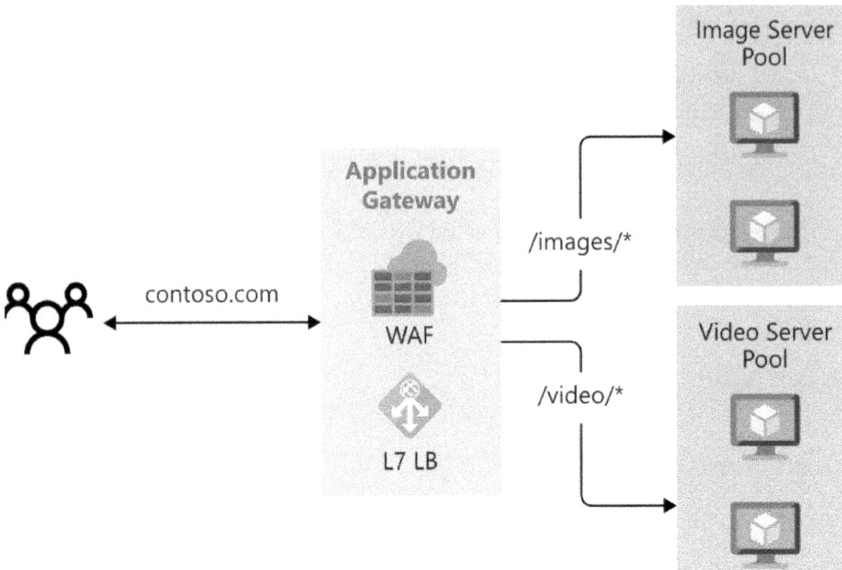

Review this website for additional information:

https://docs.microsoft.com/en-us/learn/modules/load-balance-web-traffic-with-application-gateway/2-routing-traffic-with-application-gateway

Question 42:

You need to retrieve VNet peering settings.

What is the correct PowerShell cmdlet that you can use to achieve this goal?

1. Get-AzVirtualNetworkPeering
2. Get-AzVirtualNetworkTap
3. Get-AzVirtualNetworkUsageList
4. Get-AzVirtualNetworkSubnetConfig

Explanation

Correct Answer(s): 1

Get-AzVirtualNetworkPeering

The explanation for the correct answer is:

Get-AzVirtualNetworkPeering is the correct PowerShell cmdlet to use to retrieve the Virtual Network Peerings between two networks.

Get-AzVirtualNetworkSubnetConfig - retrieves a subnet in a virtual network

Get-AzVirtualNetworkUsageList - retrieves virtual network current usage

Get-AzVirtualNetworkTap - retrieves a virtual network tap

Review this website for additional information:

https://docs.microsoft.com/en-us/powershell/module/az.network/add-azvirtualnetworkpeering

Question 43:

Review the following statement:

An Azure Site-to-Site connection requires a VPN device located on-premises that has a public IP address assigned to it and is not located behind a NAT.

Is the statement True or False?

1. TRUE
2. FALSE

Explanation

Correct Answer(s): 1

TRUE

The explanation for the correct answer is:

It is True that an Azure Site-to-Site connection requires a VPN device located on-premises that has a public IP address assigned to it and is not located behind a NAT.

Review this website for additional information:

https://docs.microsoft.com/en-us/azure/vpn-gateway/vpn-gateway-about-vpngateways#S2S

Question 44:

What protocol(s) are supported in communication for a Site-to-Site Virtual Network Gateway?

Choose the correct answer.

1. TLS
2. OpenVPN
3. SSTP
4. IPsec

Explanation

Correct Answer(s): 4

IPsec

The explanation for the correct answer is:

IPsec is the only supported in communication for a Site-to-Site Virtual Network Gateway.

SSTP and OpenVPN are supported protocols used by a Point-to-Site VPN but not a Site-to-Site VPN Gateway.

TLS is not used.

Review this website for additional information:

https://docs.microsoft.com/en-us/azure/vpn-gateway/vpn-gateway-about-vpngateways#planningtable

Question 45:

You have a policy-based VPN Gateway called CycleVPN1.

You want to change the VPN to be a route-based VPN.

Select the action that you need to take.

1. You can change the VPN to a route-based VPN from within the portal however it require a new IP address
2. You can change the VPN to a route-based VPN from within the portal however it will recreate the shared key
3. You will have to recreate the VPN with a new IP address and Pre-Shared key
4. You can change the VPN to a route-based VPN from within the portal however it will take up to 60 minutes to complete

Explanation

Correct Answer(s): 3

You will have to recreate the VPN with a new IP address and Pre-Shared key

The explanation for the correct answer is:

You cannot change the type of VPN, therefore you will have to recreate the VPN with a new IP address and Pre-Shared key.

Review this website for additional information:

https://docs.microsoft.com/en-us/azure/vpn-gateway/vpn-gateway-vpn-faq#can-i-update-my-policy-based-vpn-gateway-to-route-based

Question 46:

Review the following statement:

You can connect Virtual Networks that are in two different subscriptions.

Is the statement is TRUE or FALSE?

1. FALSE
2. TRUE

Explanation

Correct Answer(s): 2

TRUE

The explanation for the correct answer is:

TRUE - you can connect to Virtual Networks that are in different subscriptions

Review this website for additional information:

https://docs.microsoft.com/en-us/azure/vpn-gateway/vpn-gateway-vpn-faq#can-i-connect-virtual-networks-in-different-subscriptions

Question 47:

As the IT Manager at Contoso Electronics you are looking to deploy an Application Security Group within your Azure subscription.

Which of the following statements are correct about Application Security Groups?

(Select 2)

1. An Application Security Group allows you to configure network security for resources used by specific applications.
2. An Application Security Group can be used to apply a security rule to a group of resources in order to deploy and scale up specific applications workloads.
3. An Application Security Group makes administration more difficult, because you have to manually apply it to all newly created VMs.
4. Best practice is to avoid using Application Security Groups as they are often known to be complex due to how they apply to networks.

Explanation

Correct Answer(s): 1, 2

An Application Security Group allows you to configure network security for resources used by specific applications.

An Application Security Group can be used to apply a security rule to a group of resources in order to deploy and scale up specific applications workloads.

The explanation for the correct answer is:

Application Security Groups can be used to apply to a group of virtual machines or resources, no matter what the IP address or subnet. This ensures that if a new VM is deployed to this application security group it automatically picks up the security rules that have been specified.

The image gives an example of how this is used with separate VMs with both web and database roles.

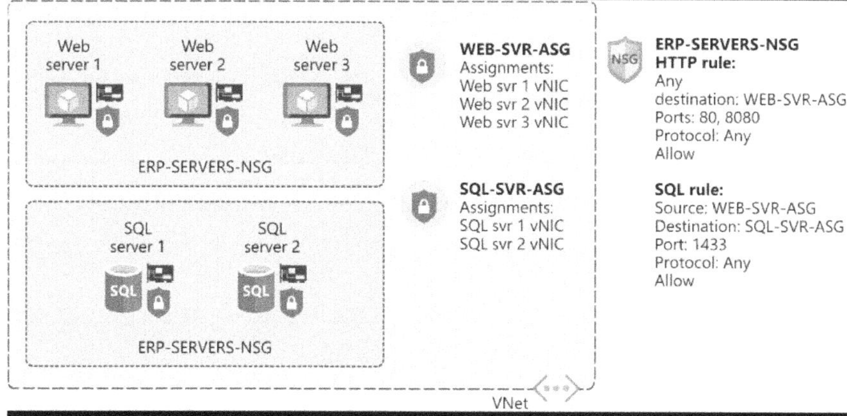

Review this website for additional information:

https://docs.microsoft.com/en-us/learn/modules/secure-and-isolate-with-nsg-and-service-endpoints/2-network-security-groups

Question 48:

A VM called bigVM01 needs to communicate with a third party SaaS application called SaaSApp1 on port 80.

The bigVM01 is unable to talk to SaaSApp1.

Select the feature of Azure Network Watcher that you should use to diagnose what might be preventing communication.

1. Next Hop
2. Security Group View
3. Network Subscription limit
4. IP Flow Verify

Explanation

Correct Answer(s): 4

IP Flow Verify

The explanation for the correct answer is:

IP Flow Verify would be the best tool to try first to diagnose any issues of this nature.

The tool will identify the security rules that are allowing or denying traffic to or from a VM.

Next Hop helps you diagnose routing problems.

Security Group View gives you a graphical network representation.

Network Subscription limit gives you metrics on the subscriptions network.

Review this website for additional information:

https://docs.microsoft.com/en-us/azure/network-watcher/diagnose-vm-network-traffic-filtering-problem#use-ip-flow-verify

Question 49:

You plan on using Flow Logs to view information about the traffic flowing through your network security groups.

However, what type of file are flow logs stored in by default?

1. XML
2. JSON
3. HTML
4. TXT
5. Azure Template

Explanation

Correct Answer(s): 2

JSON

The explanation for the correct answer is:

By default Flow Logs store data in a JSON file. Due to this it can often be difficult to find information you are looking for, especially if you have a large Azure infrastructure. This is why Power BI is quite often used to show the various traffic such as:

· Top IP Addresses

· Flows both inbound and outbound

· Flows by allowed or denied traffic

· Flows by port

Other tools can be used that are Open-source, such as Elastic Stack, Grafana or Graylog.

The image shows the workflow that an NSG uses and is then logged within the Flow Logs.

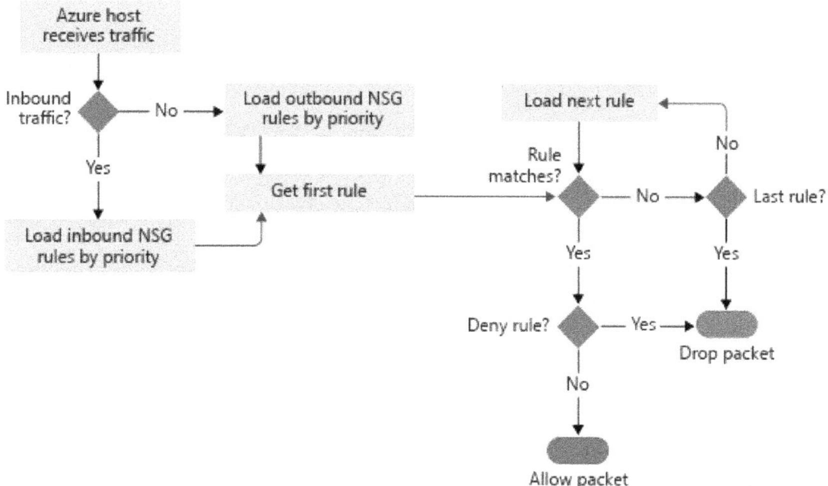

Review this website for additional information:

https://docs.microsoft.com/en-us/learn/modules/troubleshoot-azure-network-infrastructure/4-troubleshoot-networking-with-network-watcher-metrics-logs

Question 50:

You want to use Azure Network Watcher to diagnose network issues.

What do you need to configure so network monitor will work?

1. Enable OMS
2. Enable the Azure Network Watcher for your Azure region of the resources you want to "watch"
3. Setup and enable secondary NIC for any VMs requiring diagnosing
4. Add a NSG firewall to allow ICMP traffic to network watcher

Explanation

Correct Answer(s): 2

Enable the Azure Network Watcher for your Azure region of the resources you want to "watch"

The explanation for the correct answer is:

You need to enable the Azure Network Watcher for your Azure region of the resources you want to "watch".

For example if you have a VMs in East US and UK South regions then you will need to enable those regions for the network watcher.

You do not need to setup OMS, secondary NICs and an NSG for ICMP traffic.

Review this website for additional information:

https://docs.microsoft.com/en-us/azure/network-watcher/diagnose-vm-network-traffic-filtering-problem#enable-network-watcher

Question 51:

You have deployed an Azure Load Balancer that uses a backend pool that contains four virtual machines.

You notice that traffic from the load balancer is not equally being distributed across the four virtual machines.

Suggest why this is happening?

1. The load balancer is configured to use hash-based distribution mode.
2. The backend port is misconfigured in a load balancing rule.
3. The load balancer is configured to use hash-based distribution mode, but the traffic is originating from one IP address only.
4. The load balancer is configured to use source IP affinity distribution mode, but the traffic is originating from one IP address only.

Explanation

Correct Answer(s): 4

The load balancer is configured to use source IP affinity distribution mode, but the traffic is originating from one IP address only.

The explanation for the correct answer is:

The default mode for traffic distribution is 5-tuple hash-based, meaning that the following 5 factors are used:

Source IP

Source Port

Destination IP

Destination Port

Protocol

With this you would expect approximately even distribution of traffic across the backend pool.

With source IP affinity mode all traffic from the same IP address would be directed to the same backend IP address.

However, if all traffic is originating from the same IP address normally, with hash-based distribution that behaviour would not be the same and traffic would be more equally spread.

If the backend pool port was misconfigured, then no traffic would reach any backend pool server.

Review this website for additional information:

https://docs.microsoft.com/en-us/azure/load-balancer/load-balancer-distribution-mode

Question 52:

You have the following load balancing requirements:

Traffic sent to 131.107.1.200 on port 80 must be directed to VM1 or VM2.

Traffic sent to 131.107.1.200 on port 443 must be directed to VM3, VM4 or VM5.

Traffic sent to 131.107.1.100 on TCP port 12345 must be directed to a virtual machine scale set.

Traffic sent to 131.107.1.150 on TCP port 54321 must be directed to an availability set.

What is the minimum number of Azure Load Balancers do you need to create?

1. 1
2. 2
3. 3
4. 4

Explanation

Correct Answer(s): 1

1

The explanation for the correct answer is:

One is sufficient.

You can have multiple backend pools, each of which is targeted by it's own load balancing rule(s) and fronted by a different IPv4 or IPv6 address.

Review this website for additional information:

https://docs.microsoft.com/en-us/azure/load-balancer/load-balancer-multivip-overview

Question 53:

You have a virtual machine named VM3.

VM3 has a network interface that is attached to a subnet named Subnet1.

Subnet1 is part of a virtual network named VNET1.

You create a new virtual network named VNET2 and a subnet named Subnet2 in VNET2.

You need to attach VM3 to Subnet2.

What action should you perform?

1. Recreate VM3.
2. Resize VM3.
3. Add a new IP configuration to the network interface of VM3.
4. Redeploy VM3.

Explanation

Correct Answer(s): 1

Recreate VM3.

The explanation for the correct answer is:

It is not possible to move a virtual machine between subnets unless they belong to the same virtual network. You must therefore recreate VM3 to attach it to a different subnet.

Resizing can give the VM more network interfaces, but all network interfaces have to belong to the same virtual network regardless.

Redeploying a VM only makes it start on another host in the Azure fabric.

Adding a new IP (address) configuration to the existing network interface does not add it to the new virtual network/subnet.

Review this article that explains this concept further at:

https://4sysops.com/archives/move-an-azure-vm-to-another-virtual-network-vnet/

Question 54:

You want to ensure traffic doesn't route to only one application server in Azure.

You build out two identical servers hosting the same application:

Webappvm1 and Webappvm2.

How will you achieve the requirement?

1. Configure Azure fault domains
2. Configure Azure update domains
3. Configure Azure Load Balancing
4. Configure Zone Availability

Explanation

Correct Answer(s): 3

Configure Azure Load Balancing

The explanation for the correct answer is:

Azure Load Balancing will enable traffic to be balanced between the two VMs.

The other options although providing resiliency for VMs will not split traffic.

Review this website for additional information:

https://docs.microsoft.com/en-us/azure/load-balancer/load-balancer-overview

Question 55:

You are an IT Manager for Contoso Electronics. You used the Network Watcher service which returned the following error:

CPU: The connection failed because of high CPU utilisation.

Which one of the following tools, from the Network Watcher service, did you use?

1. IP Flow Verify Tool
2. Security Group View Tool
3. Packet Capture Tool
4. Connection Troubleshoot Tool
5. VPN Troubleshoot Rule
6. Next Hop Tool

Explanation

Correct Answer(s): 4

Connection Troubleshoot Tool

The explanation for the correct answer is:

The Network Watcher is a service that combines a number of different tools in a central place to diagnose the health of Azure Networks. These are specific to two categories; Monitoring Tools and Diagnostics Tools.

Within the diagnostic category are 6 tools:

IP Flow Verify Tool: This tool tells you if packets are allowed or denied for a specific VM. If a specific NSG is blocking the packet, it will tell you the name of that group so you can resolve the issue.

Next Hop Tool: With this tool you can determine how a packet gets from the source VM to any destination you specify. You will then have returned the hops, such as the virtual network gateway, that the packet travels through.

Security Group View Tool: This tool allows you to specify a VM and its network adapter and then displays all the effective NSG rules that apply to that network interface. This tool can be used to help diagnose which VM could be blocking packets.

Packet Capture Tool: This tool records all packets that are sent to and from a single VM. You can then review the information retrieved to diagnose what may have been happening. Note that this tool requires the Network Watcher Agent VM Extension to be installed on the VM.

Connection Troubleshoot Tool: This tool checks on connectivity between a source and destination VM and returns information such as latency, number of packets sent and number of hops to the destination. If the connection is not successful, there are 6 errors that it can return such as CPU, Memory, GuestFirewall, DNSResolution, NetworkSecurityRule or UserDefinedRoute.

VPN Troubleshoot Tool: This tool allows you to run diagnostics on a virtual network gateway and returns a health diagnosis. The errors can be as follows; NoFault, GatewayNotFound, PlannedMaintenance, UserDrivenUpdate, VIPUnresponsive, PlatformInActive.

Review this website for additional information:

https://docs.microsoft.com/en-us/learn/modules/troubleshoot-azure-network-infrastructure/2-troubleshoot-networking-with-network-watcher

Question 56:

Which of the following statements is true regarding Virtual Network Peering?

(Select 3)

1. In a peered virtual network you only have a single gateway, which is either local or remote when connecting to an on-premises network.
2. In a peered virtual network resources in either virtual network can directly connect with resources in the peered virtual network.
3. The traffic between a peered virtual network between VMs is routed via a gateway, or over the public internet.
4. When creating a peered virtual network there is a small amount of downtime when the connection is established.
5. When creating a peered virtual network there is no downtime when the connection is established.

Explanation

Correct Answer(s): 1, 2, 5

In a peered virtual network you only have a single gateway, which is either local or remote when connecting to an on-premises network.

In a peered virtual network resources in either virtual network can directly connect with resources in the peered virtual network.

When creating a peered virtual network there is no downtime when the connection is established.

The explanation for the correct answer is:

Because the peered virtual network is used as a transit to the on-premises network, the virtual network that is using a remote gateway can't have its own gateway. The gateway is either a local or remote gateway in the peered virtual network, as shown in the image.

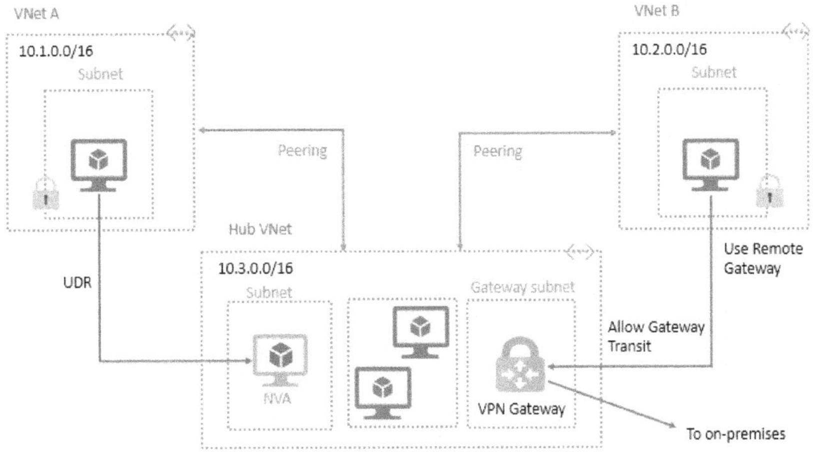

When using a peered virtual network the resources in either network are able to communicate with each other. The network latency between the VMs is the same as if they were in a single virtual network, so long as the networks are in the same region

The traffic between the VMs in a peered virtual network is routed directly through the Azure backbone infrastructure, not via a gateway or over the public internet.

Review this website for additional information:

https://docs.microsoft.com/en-us/azure/virtual-network/virtual-network-peering-overview

Question 57:

When restoring System State as files from Azure Backup, you can either:

Restore System State to the same server where the backups were taken, or Restore System State file to an alternate server.

Is this statement True or False?

1. TRUE
2. FALSE

Explanation

Correct Answer(s): 1

TRUE

The explanation for the correct answer is:

The statement is True.

When restoring System State as files from Azure Backup, you can either:

Restore System State to the same server where the backups were taken, or Restore System State file to an alternate server.

Review this website for additional information:

https://docs.microsoft.com/en-us/azure/backup/backup-azure-restore-system-state

Question 58:

Which of the following is a type of VPN is not supported by an Azure VPN Gateway?

1. site-to-site
2. point-to-site
3. network-to-network
4. point-to-network

Explanation

Correct Answer(s): 4

point-to-network

The explanation for the correct answer is:

A site-to-site VPN connects two offices in a fixed location over an untrusted network, such as the public internet, to access information in either site. With Azure, a site-to-site VPN is used to connect your on-premise location with your Azure Virtual Network.

A point-to-site VPN allows you to create a secure connection to your fixed office location, from an individual client location. This allows a remote client computer a connection to your Azure Virtual Network.

A network-to-network VPN within Azure connects two Azure Virtual Networks to each other.

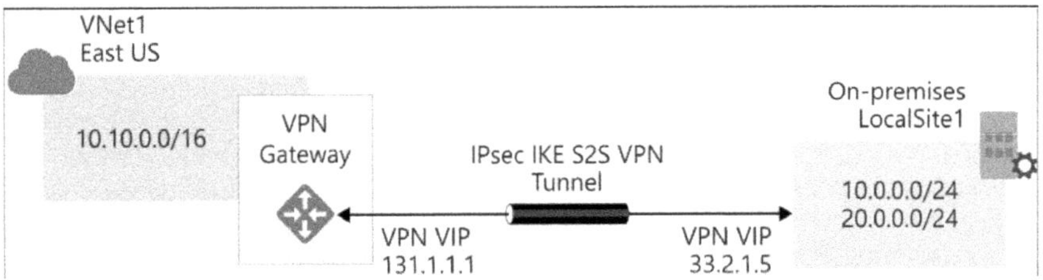

Review this website for additional information:

https://docs.microsoft.com/en-us/learn/modules/connect-on-premises-network-with-vpn-gateway/2-connect-on-premises-networks-to-azure-using-site-to-site-vpn-gateways

Question 59:

You are an IT Manager at Contoso Electronics.

You are creating a VPN in Azure, but need to ensure that the connection uses IKEv2.

Which of the following should you use?

1. Policy-Based VPN
2. Route-Based VPN

Explanation

Correct Answer(s): 2

Route-Based VPN

The explanation for the correct answer is:

Policy-based VPNs ONLY support IKEv1, therefore if you are wanting a connection that supports IKEv2.. You should use a Route-Based VPN.

Policy-based VPNs are usually used in a legacy environment where the on-premises VPN requires older compatibility.

The images give examples of both a Policy-Based VPN and a Route-Based VPN

Policy-Based VPN:

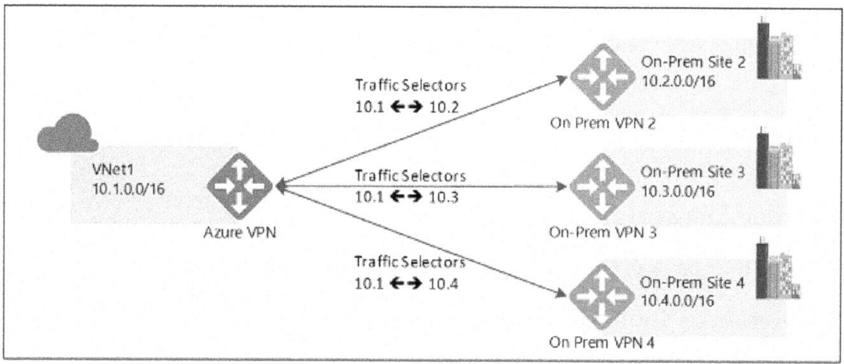

Route-based VPN:

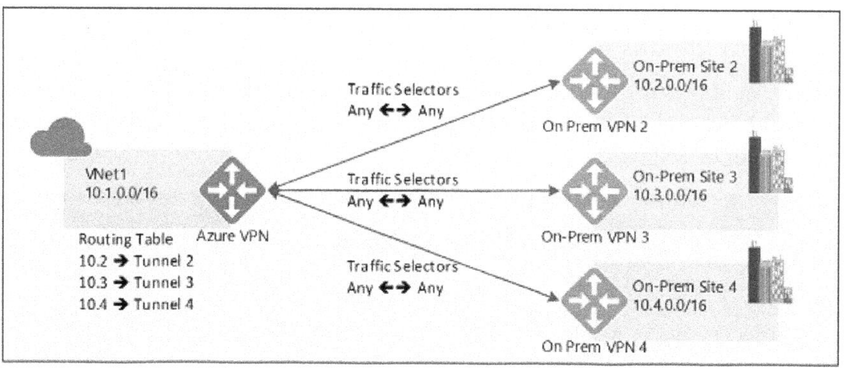

Review this website for additional information:

https://docs.microsoft.com/en-us/learn/modules/connect-on-premises-network-with-vpn-gateway/2-connect-on-premises-networks-to-azure-using-site-to-site-vpn-gateways

Question 60:

You are an IT Manager at Contoso Electronics.

You have previously deployed a Basic VPN Gateway in order to test that the connection works before deploying to the other users.

You need to ensure that the new connection supports throughput up to 1Gbps.

Which of the following is the correct step?

1. Migrate from Basic to the VpnGw2/Az SKU
2. Migrate from Basic to the VpnGw1/Az SKU
3. Remove the Gateway and create a new one with the VpnGw2/Az SKU
4. Remove the Gateway and create a new one with the VpnGw1/Az SKU

Explanation

Correct Answer(s): 3

Remove the Gateway and create a new one with the VpnGw2/Az SKU

The explanation for the correct answer is:

The Basic SKU when creating a VPN Gateway is only meant to be used for Dev/Test workloads. It is also unsupported to migrate from Basic to any of the VpnGwX/Az SKUs. Meaning that you would have to remove and redeploy the VPN Gateway.

The image shows the throughput benchmark of each of the VPN Gateway SKUs – VpnGw1/Az only has a throughput of 650Mbps whereas VpnGw2/Az has throughput of 1Gbps.

SKU	Site-to-site/VNet-to-VNet tunnels	Aggregate throughput benchmark	Border Gateway Protocol (BGP) support
Basic*	Maximum: 10	100 Mbps	Not supported
VpnGw1/Az	Maximum: 30	650 Mbps	Supported
VpnGw2/Az	Maximum: 30	1 Gbps	Supported
VpnGw3/Az	Maximum: 30	1.25 Gbps	Supported

Review this website for additional information:

https://docs.microsoft.com/en-us/learn/modules/connect-on-premises-network-with-vpn-gateway/2-connect-on-premises-networks-to-azure-using-site-to-site-vpn-gateways

Question 61:

What Azure CLI cmdlet should you run to stop a running Azure Backup job?

1. az backup job stop
2. az backup job start
3. az backup job wait
4. az backup job quit

Explanation

Correct Answer(s): 1

az backup job stop

The explanation for the correct answer is:

az backup job stop is the correct AZ CLI command to stop a running Azure backup job.

az backup job start and az backup job quit are not valid Azure CLI commands.

az backup job wait - is incorrect, this will wait until either the job completes or the specified timeout value is reached.

Review this website for additional information:

https://docs.microsoft.com/en-gb/cli/azure/backup/job?view=azure-cli-latest#commands

Question 62:

What task does the following Azure CLI script perform?

1. Creates a recovery services vault with the progress outputted to a table
2. Outputs the restore jobs with their progress to a table
3. Starts a full recovery point backup job with the progress outputted to a table
4. Enables backup for an Azure VM and confirms the result in a table

Explanation

Correct Answer(s): 2

Outputs the restore jobs with their progress to a table

The explanation for the correct answer is:

The script allows you to monitor the status of backup jobs.

The az backup job list cmdlet produces an output is similar to the following example, which shows the backup job is InProgress:

Name Operation Status Item Name Start Time UTC Duration

-------- --------------- ---------- ----------- ------------------- --------------

a0a8e5e6 Backup InProgress myvm 2017-09-19T03:09:21 0:00:48.718366

fe5d0414 ConfigureBackup Completed myvm 2017-09-19T03:03:57 0:00:31.191807

Review this website for additional information:

https://docs.microsoft.com/en-us/azure/backup/quick-backup-vm-cli

Question 63:

Review the following statement:

In Azure Site Recovery there are compute costs for performing DR drills.

Is the statement True or False?

1. TRUE
2. FALSE

Explanation

Correct Answer(s): 2

FALSE

The explanation for the correct answer is:

There is no separate cost for to perform disaster recovery (DR) drills/test failover.

There will be compute charges after the VM is created after the test failover.

Review this website for additional information:

https://docs.microsoft.com/en-us/azure/site-recovery/site-recovery-faq#is-there-a-cost-associated-to-perform-disaster-recovery-drillstest-failover

Question 64:

You need to configure Azure Backup reports so you can check backup success of your estate.

In configuring the Diagnostic Logging for these reports, select the location where can you will archive the backup reports.

1. Local Log files
2. Azure Security Center
3. Storage Account
4. Event Hub

Explanation

Correct Answer(s): 3

Storage Account

The explanation for the correct answer is:

The correct answer is to store them in a Storage Account.

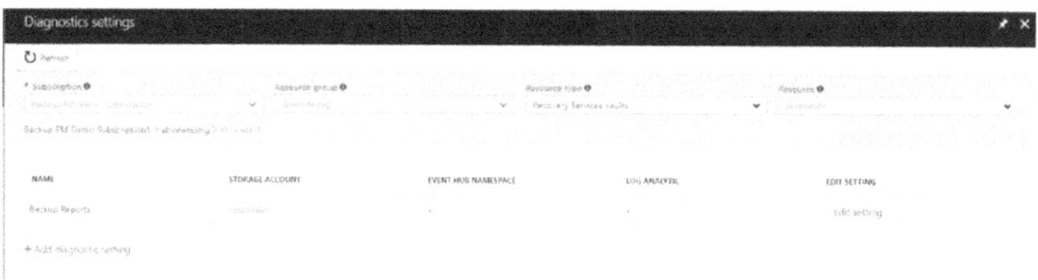

After the Storage Account is configured, you can additionally stream the logs to view them in Power BI or send them to Log Analytics.

Review this website for additional information:

https://docs.microsoft.com/en-us/azure/backup/backup-azure-configure-reports

Question 65:

You have configured the Azure Backup Microsoft Azure Recovery Services to back up your Azure IaaS servers.

Your organization requirements include performing a number of backups throughout the day.

What is the maximum number of backups that you can perform each day?

1. 1
2. 3
3. 6
4. 24

Explanation

Correct Answer(s): 2

3

The explanation for the correct answer is:

With the Azure Backup Microsoft Azure Recovery Services (MARS) you are limited to a maximum of 3 backups per day.

Review this website for additional information:

https://docs.microsoft.com/en-us/azure/backup/backup-introduction-to-azure-backup#which-azure-backup-components-should-i-use

Question 66:

You work for Cycleshare.com as a Cloud Administrator.

Cycleshare.com has an estate of 60 Virtual Machines on-premises and in also located in Azure.

Cycleshare.com have Azure Backup in place and this is used to backup existing servers using the MARS agent.

You need to backup new services and VMs that have been deployed.

Which of the following servers and services can be backed up using the existing backup solution?

(Select all that apply.)

1. Microsoft SharePoint Server in Azure
2. Windows 2016 File Server on-premises (hosted on Hyper-V)
3. Windows 2012 R2 SQL Server in Azure
4. Windows 2019 Server VM (Hosted on VMware)
5. Linux VM on-premises (hosted on Hyper-V)

Explanation

Correct Answer(s): 1, 2

Windows 2016 File Server on-premises (hosted on Hyper-V)

Microsoft SharePoint Server in Azure

The explanation for the correct answer is:

Microsoft SharePoint Server in Azure and Windows 2016 File Server on-premises (hosted on Hyper-V) can be used with Azure Backup Microsoft Azure Recovery Services (MARS) and the MARS agent.

The following servers cannot be backed up with Azure Backup MARS:

Linux VM on-premises (hosted on Hyper-V)

Windows 2019 Server VM (Hosted on VMware)

Windows 2012 R2 SQL Server in Azure

To back up these types of servers you would require Microsoft DPM or an Azure Backup Server (MABS v3).

Review these websites for additional information:

https://docs.microsoft.com/en-us/azure/backup/backup-configure-vault

https://docs.microsoft.com/en-us/azure/backup/backup-introduction-to-azure-backup#which-azure-backup-components-should-i-use

Question 67:

Which of the following operating systems can be backed up with Azure Backup?

(Select all that apply.)

1. Windows 7 64 bit
2. Windows 2019 Essentials Server 64 bit
3. Windows 2016 Server 64 bit

4. Windows 2003 Server
5. Windows 2008 R2 Server 32 bit
6. Windows XP 32 bit

Explanation

Correct Answer(s): 1, 2, 3

Windows 7 64 bit

Windows 2019 Essentials Server 64 bit

Windows 2016 Server 64 bit

The explanation for the correct answer is:

Azure Backup supports the following operating systems:

Windows 2016 Server 64 bit

Windows 7 64 bit

Windows 2019 Essentials 64 bit

Windows XP and Windows Server 2003 and 32 bit operating systems are not supported.

Review this website for additional information:

https://docs.microsoft.com/en-us/azure/backup/backup-azure-backup-faq#what-operating-systems-are-supported-for-backup

Question 68:

What is the maximum limit of Azure Virtual Machines that can be registered in an Azure Recovery Services Vault?

1. 100
2. 1000
3. 250
4. 50

Explanation

Correct Answer(s): 2

1000

The explanation for the correct answer is:

You can register up to 1000 Azure Virtual Machines per Azure Recovery Services Vault.

Review this website for additional information:

https://docs.microsoft.com/en-us/azure/backup/backup-azure-backup-faq#recovery-services-vault

Question 69:

The DevOps manager of Cycleshare.com asks you to ensure that a critical WebApp called CycleApp1 is monitored.

DevOps engineers must receive an email whenever CycleApp1 stops for any reason.

What should you configure to fulfil this requirement?

(Choose the best option.)

1. Create Diagnostic Logs for the WebApp by configuring a resource, condition and action group.
2. Create an Alert for the WebApp by configuring a resource, condition, action group and alert details.
3. Create Resource Health for the WebApp by configuring a resource, condition and action group.
4. Create an Alert for the WebApp by configuring a resource, condition, alert group and alert details.

Explanation

Correct Answer(s): 2

Create an Alert for the WebApp by configuring a resource, condition, action group and alert details.

The explanation for the correct answer is:

To alert DevOps engineers whenever CycleApp1 stops for any reason, you need to configure an Alert for the WebApp by configuring a resource, condition, action group and alert details.

Review this website for additional information:

https://docs.microsoft.com/en-us/azure/app-service/web-sites-monitor

Question 70:

You have a VM called "Webapp01" and you want to view resource usage for the VM for the previous week.

What should you configure to provide you with this information?

Select all that apply.

1. Azure Crash Dump Logger
2. Azure Monitoring Metrics
3. Azure Monitoring Insights
4. Azure Monitoring Alerts
5. Azure VM Boot Diagnostics

Explanation

Correct Answer(s): 2, 3

Azure Monitoring Metrics

Azure Monitoring Insights

The explanation for the correct answer is:

Configuring Azure Monitoring Metrics or Azure Monitoring Insights will give you performance data that you require for the VM. Azure Crash Dump Logger is not a valid Azure service.

Azure Monitoring Alerts is configured to give you alerting rather than metrics.

Azure VM Boot Diagnostics provides diagnostics into VM Boot issues or crashes.

Review this website for additional information:

https://docs.microsoft.com/en-us/azure/virtual-machines/windows/monitor

Question 71:

You are the administrator of CycleShare.com.

You are configuring diagnostic logging in Azure for a VM called "CycleDiag1".

When you are configuring a Sink what Azure service can you output to?

1. Azure Security Center
2. Application Insights
3. Azure Operations Manager
4. Azure Storage Account

Explanation

Correct Answer(s): 2

Application Insights

The explanation for the correct answer is:

You need to configure a Sink to Application Insights for application layer information.

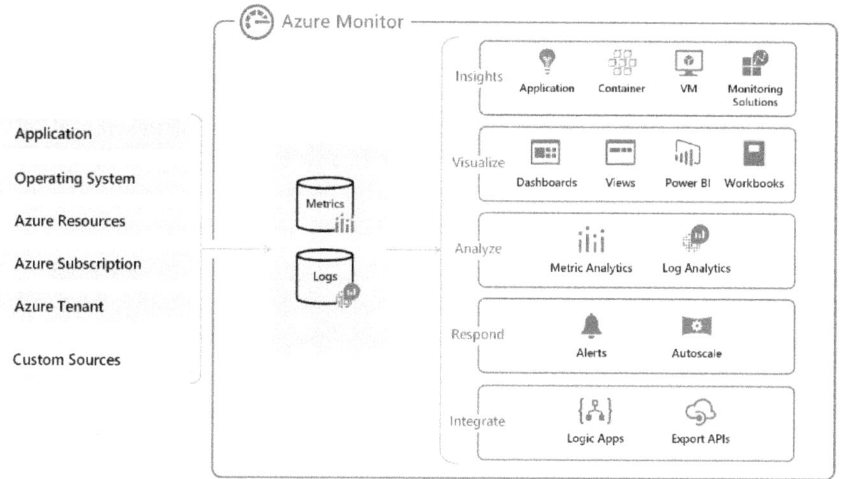

Azure Security Center is for security issues or risks across your environment.

You can't configure a Storage Account as a Sink.

Azure OMS isn't the best fit solution.

Review this website for additional information:

https://docs.microsoft.com/en-gb/azure/azure-monitor/platform/data-platform?toc=%2Fazure%2Fazure-monitor%2Ftoc.json

Question 72:

Examine the following PowerShell script and choose the option that completes the statement to configure Diagnostic logs to stream to event hub.

Set-AzDiagnosticSetting -ResourceId logsbapp01 -ServiceBusRuleId serbuazh740

1. /Start
2. -Begin
3. -Enabled $true
4. -Enable

Explanation

Correct Answer(s):

-Enabled $true

The explanation for the correct answer is:

The correct full PowerShell script is:

Set-AzDiagnosticSetting -ResourceId logsbapp01 -ServiceBusRuleId serbuazh740 -Enabled $true

Review this website for additional information:

https://docs.microsoft.com/en-us/azure/azure-monitor/platform/diagnostic-logs-overview

Question 73:

What action can you not configure with an Alert rule?

(Select all that apply.)

1. SCOM Alert
2. SMS
3. Email
4. Webhook

5. Logic App

Explanation

Correct Answer(s): 1

SCOM Alert

The explanation for the correct answer is:

The only action you cannot configure with an alert is a SCOM Alert.

The following are all actions that can be configured in Azure alerts:

SMS

Email

Webhook

Logic App

Review this website for additional information:

https://docs.microsoft.com/en-us/azure/app-service/web-sites-monitor

Question 74:

What is the default retention period for Azure Activity logs?

1. 30 days
2. 90 days
3. 60 days
4. 120 days

Explanation

Correct Answer(s): 2

90 days

The explanation for the correct answer is:

Activity logs are kept for 90 days.

To store them for a longer period, you can keep them in Activity Monitor and export them to an Event Hub.

Review this website for additional information:

https://docs.microsoft.com/en-us/azure/azure-monitor/platform/activity-logs-overview#activity-log-retention

Question 75:

You have a Resource Group in your subscription named RG1.

RG1 contains a Recovery Services vault that contains protected items.

You attempt to delete RG1 and the task fails.

You need to recommend a solution that allows RG1 to be deleted.

1. Delete the virtual machines that are protected by the Recovery Services vault, then delete RG1.
2. Delete the Recovery Services vault, then delete RG1.
3. Delete the protected items from the Recovery Services vault. Remove the vault, then remove RG1.
4. Modify the role assignments on RG1.

Explanation

Correct Answer(s): 3

Delete the protected items from the Recovery Services vault. Remove the vault, then remove RG1.

The explanation for the correct answer is:

Certain resources will block a Resource Group from being deleted.

A Recovery Services vault contains backup data from virtual machines, so you must manually delete that content first before the vault and finally the Resource Group can be deleted.

You cannot delete a Recovery Services vault that has dependencies such as protected servers, virtual machines or backup management servers associated with the vault. Vault containing backup data cannot be deleted.

Review this website for additional information:

https://docs.microsoft.com/en-us/azure/backup/backup-azure-delete-vault

Question 76:

Which of the following statements regarding Azure Backup are true?

(Select 4)

1. Azure Backup can only be used to backup once every 24 hours
2. Azure Backup has a number of configuration steps and is difficult to set-up
3. Azure Backup uses an agent installed on the physical or virtual machine, or can be used as part of a dedicated backup server
4. Azure Backup can be used to backup the entire VM, files and folders, or running apps
5. Azure Backup can only backup the OS Disk on the VM
6. Azure Backup does not support Linux
7. Azure Backup uses a Recovery Services Vault to manage and store the backup data in Azure
8. Azure Backup pricing is based on the size of the backed-up data and begins as soon as the first backup is completed

Explanation

Correct Answer(s): 3, 4, 7, 8

Azure Backup uses an agent installed on the physical or virtual machine, or can be used as part of a dedicated backup server

Azure Backup can be used to backup the entire VM, files and folders, or running apps

Azure Backup uses a Recovery Services Vault to manage and store the backup data in Azure

Azure Backup pricing is based on the size of the backed-up data and begins as soon as the first backup is completed

The explanation for the correct answer is:

Azure Backup is easily configurable. It has options for backup times (which can be set as required, not just once a day!), retention periods and you are able to select what you want to backup. This can include the entire VM, files and folder or any running apps.

Azure Backup also supports both Windows and Linux OS.

The below image shows the various options available when configuring retention options within Azure Backup.

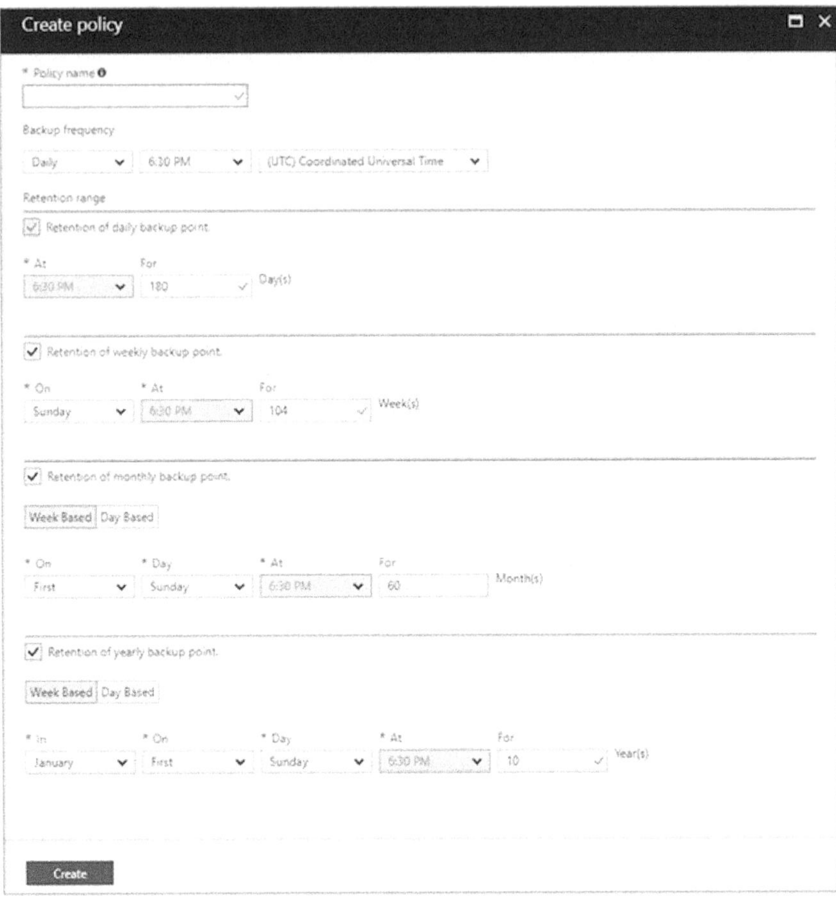

Review this website for additional information:

https://docs.microsoft.com/en-us/learn/modules/protect-virtual-machines-with-azure-backup/3-back-up-azure-virtual-machine

Question 77:

You are the Database Administrator for Contoso Electronics and need to ensure that the databases stored in Azure are backed up and can be restored quickly in the event of a disaster.

Which of the following statements relating to Azure Backup for Azure SQL Databases are true?

(Select 3)

1. The default retention period when you create a database for a Standard tier is 5 weeks
2. The default retention period when you create a database for a Basic tier is 5 weeks
3. The default retention period when you create a database for a Premium tier is 7 weeks.
4. When an Azure SQL Backup job is created it will automatically start at midnight of the following day.
5. There are three types of backups that can be configured; Full Backup, Differential Backup and Transactional Backup.
6. There are currently only two types of backup types that can be configured; Full Backup and Transactional Backup.
7. Azure SQL Backup is not encrypted automatically.
8. Azure SQL Backup is encrypted automatically.

Explanation

Correct Answer(s): 1, 5, 8

The default retention period when you create a database for a Standard tier is 5 weeks.

There are three types of backups that can be configured; Full Backup, Differential Backup and Transactional Backup.

Azure SQL Backup is encrypted automatically.

The explanation for the correct answer is:

By default, the retention period for a Basic Service tier is 1 week. Comparatively, Standard and Premium tiers both have a default retention period of 5 weeks. You can however change that period from 0 to 35 days once the backup has been configured.

Azure SQL Backups will start as soon as the job has been configured and usually finishes within 30 minutes of the backup being started.

Azure SQL Backups can be Full, Differential or Transactional. A Full back contains everything in the database and the transaction logs. This occurs once a week. A differential backup includes all changes since the last full backup. This occurs every 12 hours. A Transactional Backup includes the contents of all the transaction logs in the database. A Transactional backup occurs every 5-10 minutes, which enables Administrators to restore up to a specific time, e.g. the moment before data is deleted.

Azure SQL Backup is encrypted before it leaves the source database, whether it is in transit or held in the Azure Backup Vault.

Review this website for additional information:

https://docs.microsoft.com/en-us/learn/modules/backup-restore-azure-sql/2-protect-database-with-backup

Question 78:

You are the IT Manager at Contoso Electronics.

You notice that every Thursday evening the system has severe performance related issues and users are unable to work as expected.

You decide to enable and configure the Azure Diagnostics Extension. Which of the following metrics can be enabled?

(Choose 5)

1. Processor
2. Disk
3. Filesystem
4. Start-up Settings
5. Network
6. Memory
7. Temperature

Explanation

Correct Answer(s): 1, 2, 3, 5, 6

Processor

Memory

Network

Filesystem

Disk

The explanation for the correct answer is:

Processor, Memory, Network, Filesystem and Disk are all metrics that can enabled within the Diagnostic settings panel of Azure. Each of these features provides specific information that you can then choose to meet your needs.

When you have enabled and collected the diagnostics logs for a VM, you are able to keep that information in a variety of places – see image.

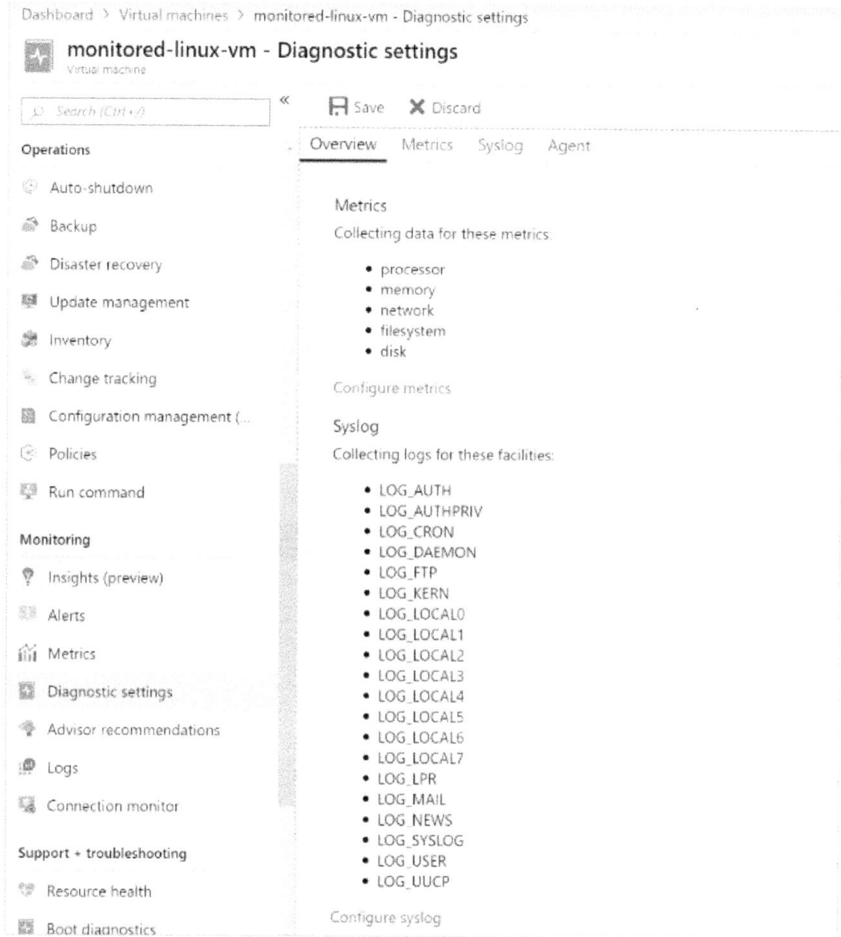

Review this website for additional information:

https://docs.microsoft.com/en-us/learn/modules/monitor-azure-vm-using-diagnostic-data/5-configure-azure-diagnostic-extension

Question 79:

You need to ensure that all alerts and notifications from the Azure Security Center are sent directly to the IT Helpdesk.

Which of the following modules within the Azure Security Center should be used to ensure this is possible?

1. Just-In-Time Access
2. Advanced Cloud Defense
3. Playbooks
4. Adaptive Application Controls

Explanation

Correct Answer(s): 3

Playbooks

The explanation for the correct answer is:

Just-In-Time virtual machine access is a feature that ensures all access is audited and only granted when configured. The image shows a list of the default ports that Just-In-Time will target, as well as allows you to configure ones yourself.

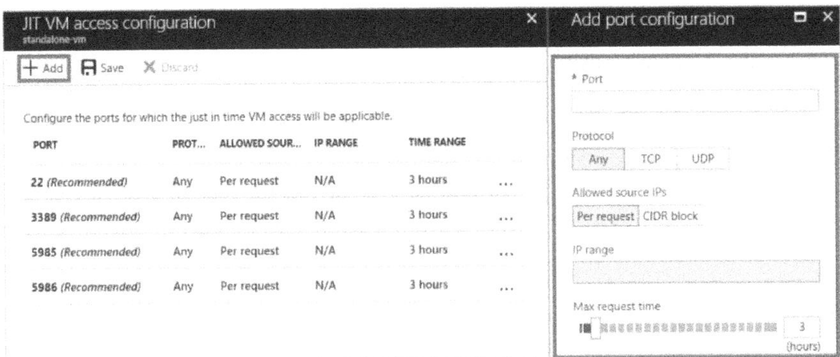

Playbooks allow you to automatically run procedures against alerts. For instance, you can configure a playbook to automatically e-mail when a potential SQL injection is recognised on your Azure VM.

Advanced Cloud Defense is the module within Azure Security Center that you can enable Just-In-Time as per the explanation above.

Within the Advanced Cloud Defense section of the Azure Security Center, you can configure Adaptive Application Controls which allows you to set certain policies against VMs on what happens to malicious software.

Review this website for additional information:

https://docs.microsoft.com/en-us/learn/modules/design-monitoring-strategy-on-azure/4-security-center

Question 80:

Azure Monitor is a service that allows you to gain insights and analyse performance data of your infrastructure and applications.

This for both in the cloud and on-premises infrastructure and applications.

Which two fundamental types of data does Azure Monitor collect?

1. Metrics & Logs
2. Diagnostic & Performance
3. Packet Capture & Network Performance

Explanation

Correct Answer(s): 1

Metrics & Logs

The explanation for the correct answer is:

Azure Monitor has a number of features that allow you to ensure that your resource is performing as expected, as well as what resources it is using which then allows you to control costs etc. The image shows the process that Azure monitor uses and what can happen to that data as soon as it has been collected in near-real time.

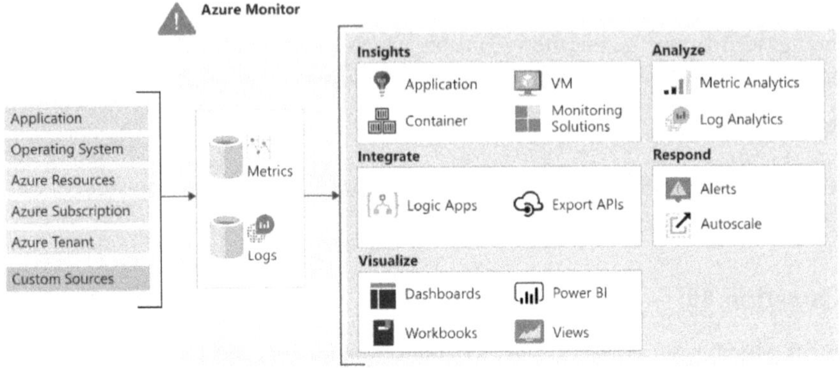

Review this website for additional information:

https://docs.microsoft.com/en-us/learn/modules/analyze-infrastructure-with-azure-monitor-logs/2-features-azure-monitor-log

Question 81:

You need to ensure that in the event of a disaster you are able to recover with the shortest time possible and meet your Recovery Time Objective (RTO).

You are going to use the Azure Site Recovery within Azure to do a test failover to ensure everything works as expected.

Which of the below steps are correct?

1. Select the VM > Restore > Select Date > Confirm
2. Site Recovery > Recovery Plans > Recovery Plan Name > Test Failover
3. Site Recovery > Test Failover > Recovery Plan Names
4. Select the VM > Jobs > Recovery > Recovery Plan > Restore

Explanation

Correct Answer(s): 2

Site Recovery > Recovery Plans > Recovery Plan Name > Test Failover

The explanation for the correct answer is:

In order to test the Recovery Plan that has already been created you must go into Site Recovery, select your plan and Test Failover. It is important to ensure that on the following steps you use an isolated network from the live environment to prevent any impact to the production environment.

You are able to track that recovery within the 'Jobs' section of the Site Recovery dashboard.

The image shows the various options available on the Site Recovery dashboard.

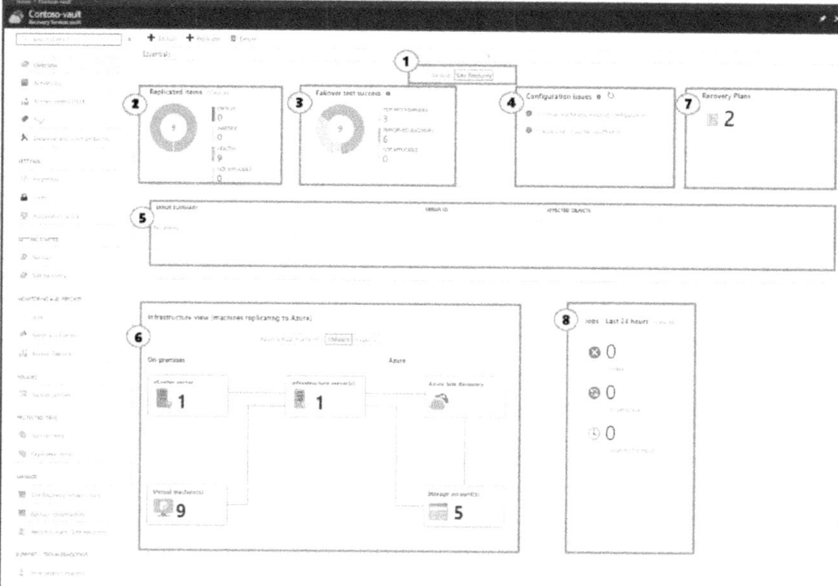

Review this website for additional information:

https://docs.microsoft.com/en-us/learn/modules/protect-on-premises-infrastructure-with-azure-site-recovery/4-run-disaster-recovery-drill

Question 82:

You are an IT Manager for Contoso Electronics.

You are going to upgrade one of your business critical applications and need to ensure a backup is taken first. You plan on performing an on-demand backup job outside of your normal scheduled backup.

What will the retention period of this backup be by default?

1. The same as your normal backup policy used in scheduled backups
2. 30 days
3. 60 days
4. 120 days

Explanation

Correct Answer(s): 2

30 days

The explanation for the correct answer is:

When an on-demand backup job is performed the default retention Is 30 days when triggered via the Azure portal. You can however specify other retention options if required.

Review this website for additional information:

https://docs.microsoft.com/en-us/azure/backup/backup-azure-vm-backup-faq

www.ingramcontent.com/pod-product-compliance
Ingram Content Group UK Ltd.
Pitfield, Milton Keynes, MK11 3LW, UK
UKHW021913190726
13853UKWH00002B/649